I am a Happy Theologian

I am a Happy Theologian

Conversations with Francesco Strazzari

Edward Schillebeeckx

SCM PRESS LTD

Translated by John Bowden from the Italian *Sono Un Teologo Felice. Colloqui con Francesco Strazzari*, published 1993 by Edizioni Dehoniane, Bologna.

0 334 00747 X

230·2   20026898

First British edition published 1994
by SCM Press Ltd,
26-30 Tottenham Road, London N1 4BZ

Phototypeset by Intype, London and
Printed and bound in Great Britain by
Mackays of Chatham PLC, Chatham, Kent

Contents

Introduction

Honest to the World
The Frontier Theology of
Edward Schillebeeckx

ROSINO GIBELLINI

According to the philosopher Martin Heidegger, every great thinker is always guided by a single thought which is expressed in manifold variations. If that is true, it can be said that the leading thought of the theological research and reflection of Edward Schillebeeckx is a frontier problem, namely the relationship between Christian experience and human experience. A Flemish-speaking Belgian theologian, teaching theology first at Louvain in Belgium and then (from 1958) in the theological faculty of the Catholic University of Nijmegen in the Netherlands, Schillebeeckx began to become a firm fixture in the panorama of the church and theology in the first half of the 1960s, at the time of the Second Vatican Council, in which he took part as a theological consultant to the then dynamic Dutch episcopate. One of the most innovative themes of the Council which, to give it the title used then, went under the name of 'church and world' found in the lectures and articles of this northern theologian the most sensitive and most acute of interpreters. This was documented in a series of volumes which in the Netherlands bore the general title 'Theological Soundings' (5 vols., 1964-1972: see the bibliography on p. 84f.). These volumes brought together the many essays in which he commented both on the conciliar debate and on the international theological debate.

We can distinguish two periods in the work of Edward Schillebeeckx (who was born in 1914). In the first, which is to be put between the beginnings of his academic activity immediately after the Second World War, in 1946, and the period immediately after the Council, in 1966-1967, his reflections follow the lines of an open Thomism: studies from this first period include his work on the theology of the sacraments, represented by his historical reconstruction of sacramental theology in *The Sacramental Economy of Salvation* (1952, a book which was never translated into English) and the subsequent systematic treatment in *Christ the Sacrament* (1958). The writings of this period are characterized by the historical method, which reconstructs the history of the doctrine before going on to a systematic development. This was a method which Schillebeeckx learned in the school of Le Saulchoir and at the École des Hautes Études of the Sorbonne (where the ex-Director of Le Saulchoir, Marie-Dominique Chenu, was giving specialist courses). His approach was also characterized by the gnoseological perspectivism which he learned at Louvain in the school of De Petter, who presented a synthesis of Thomism and phenomenology.

In the second period, which began immediately after the Council and found first expression in the American lectures of 1967, *God, The Future of Man*, there was a 'notable change' – to use a phrase of the North American theologian Robert Schreiter, a former pupil of Schillebeeckx at Nijmegen and one of the experts on his theology. From then on there was a shift which led the Dominican theologian to abandon the scholastic Thomism (even as reinterpreted by his Louvain teachers) which represented the conceptual frame of reference for his earlier works, to tackle the new hermeneutics, and to enter into a more direct dialogue with the experience of modern secular men and women and the contemporary world. In this second period, the more original and creative, the Nijmegen theologian came to grips with the hermeneutical problem, introduced it into Catholic systematic theology, and applied it radically and with rigour to the very heart of theological discussion, i.e. to christology.

Hermeneutical theory raises the problem of interpretation, namely, the intelligibility of the texts of revelation, their message for the present and the relevance of the formulas of faith for experience. It had made its way into Protestant theology with the hermeneutics of Schleiermacher, and decisively in this century with the existential hermeneutics of Fuchs and Ebeling in the 1940s and 1950s. The purpose of Schillebeeckx's hermeneutical essays – collected in the fifth volume of his 'Theological Soundings' under the title *The Understanding of Faith* (1972) – is to offer a contribution to the introduction of hermeneutics in Catholic systematic theology.

Post-conciliar Catholic theology, which began to face up to secular culture, took account of the fact that there are two sources of theological reflection: revelation and Christian tradition on the one hand and human experience on the other. The hermeneutical work to be done is achieve a constant correlation between the two sources (or the two poles) of Christian faith and human experience. But faith itself, as adherence to revelation (the first source of theology), has an experiential structure: faith is an *experience*, an experience with *experiences*, namely *Christian* experience of *human* experiences (the experience of themselves and the world that Christians have as human beings). In the beginning there is not a doctrine; rather, 'I begin with a very precise experience', which has set in motion a continuing 'history of experiences'.

In fact at the beginning of the New Testament there is an encounter between Jesus and his disciples who, in this encounter, which was disturbing and overwhelming, had an experience of salvation which they then interpreted and set down in writing. The interpretation is also part of the experience, in that any experience contains interpretative elements; it is an interpretative perception. In the end, the New Testament is the account of an interpreted experience of salvation: the experience comes down to a message, and the message is transmitted by generating a living experience in the hearer. The message refers to an experience as its origin and activates an experience as its result. To begin with, the divine revelation is not a doctrine, but the free initiative of God which communicates itself by manifesting itself in facts which determine an experience of salvation that is interpreted and fixed in a written message. The message contains a doctrine; however, the doctrine is not the primary element, but the experience. The doctrine is like a rearrangement at the level of reflection, deepens the experiential content which comes at the beginning, and serves to transmit and activate such an experience of salvation. So it takes its place in the living Christian tradition by creating an experience: in the end we have a Christian story of continuing experience.

Now because this is a *continuing* Christian story of experience, the message which is transmitted must be comprehensible to men and women of today. It is not just to be accepted on the basis of an institutional authority which mediates it. In secular society religious experience is no longer a high experience, a widely generalized experience, but takes the form of an 'experience with experiences'. So it must find a place in the context of secular human experiences if it is to be convincing to personal experience. The message of the tradition must be presented in a 'catechesis of experience' as a possible interpretation of human experiences, as a 'research project' which investigates the meaning of being human; it must be capable of being experimented with as a 'response of liberation' to the vital questions posed by human beings. Theology is called to keep open the communication between the traditional content of faith and human experience, in a constant critical correlation between the two sources, biblical tradition (the first source) and our current world of experience and faith (second source).

Schillebeeckx has tackled this task in a vast 'christological project' in three thick volumes: *Jesus* (1974), which analyses the basic Christian experience in the Synoptic current; *Christ* (1977), which analyses the basic Christian experience in the other New Testament currents, in particular in the Pauline and Johannine writings, and in a suggestive final synthesis identifies some structural elements of the christological tradition of the church and secular human experience; and *Church* (1989), which shows how the heart of the Christian message, salvation in Jesus from God, can be experienced anew in the history of humanity.

These three volumes by the Nijmegen theologian represent the broadest and most creative christological work of our century. Its methodology is innovative: Schillebeeckx does not follow the guiding thread of the church's tradition (as is usual in christological treatises), but accepts the challenge of radical negations, using the historical-critical method in a radical way. He aims to adopt the most uncompromising historical approach possible, but behind his historical research is the theological purpose of reconstructing the genesis of the church's christological confession and showing that it is also relevant to our contemporaries in the secular city. The method is intrinsically legitimate and does not lead to a radicalization of the substance of christology; the discussion which followed – at the official level as well – related only to some features of the way in which he carried out what can be called a real 'experiment in christology'.

Schillebeeckx does not accept that secularization invalidates theological discussion, in that the self-understanding of secular men and women remains open to the mystery, as can be proved from their radical trust in reality, their commitment to others, and their concern to do good and fight against evil. Rather, secularization relocates theological discourse, and the task of hermeneutics is to help to determine a situation which allows the secular self-understanding to transcend itself and to open itself to the mystery of life and reality, which has been decisively and definitively revealed in the figure of Christ. The assertions of faith and theological propositions cannot be deduced from experience, but must have the backing of experience, or must be in a position to illuminate experience, to speak to the experience of secular men and women; otherwise they cannot be defended and communication is broken off.

To achieve this, theology must constantly correlate the response of faith with the human question, which draws on experience. And this correlation comes about if the human question can be framed as a *question about the meaning* of reality and existence, followed by *human responses* which try to articulate a meaning but which only from the *Christian response* receive a superabundance of meaning, an ultimate and definitive meaning. The Christian response is, then, the definitive response to the human question, which is articulated in a radical question and partial responses. Only faith gives a radical response to the radical question about humanity. However, the Christian response does not fall vertically from above, but inserts itself into a context of experiences in which meaning is acquired, giving a superabundance of meaning. And this superabundance of meaning must not only demonstrate itself in theory but also descend to the level of practice. In this sense one can talk of a 'hermeneutic of experience and praxis'.

Schillebeeckx's theology does not seek to oppose and to challenge secular culture – this is the attitude of fundamentalist religious thought, including that of a Catholic kind – but to make itself part of the human quest, to be aware of the many different anthropological projects which are being developed in secular culture, and which, if only in their fragmentation, prove to be a thematization of the universal experience of a quest for meaning that relates to the horizon of a full humanity, which is the horizon of faith.

Here, then, is a theology which has a lively sense of the integrity of the *humanum* in its anthropological, social and cultural, theoretical and practical, utopian and religious dimensions. It is a theology which develops a soteriology in a modern key, in that it is guided by two preoccupations: in the negative sense, by what Bloch calls the 'threatened *humanum*' and by the stories of the suffering and death of men and women; and in a positive sense by what Ricoeur calls the 'desirable *humanum*', the fullness and integrity of the *humanum*. Both preoccupations are shared, at their level, by the secular movements of emancipation and liberation, but they find in Christian salvation a radicality and fullness of interpretations and of meaning. One cannot talk of Christian salvation if one skips over, censures or denigrates the history of human emancipation and liberation in order to get to religious salvation. What unifies culture in the modern and contemporary eras is the quest not for an exclusively religious salvation, as could happen in past eras, but for a healthy humanity with integrity, which makes life worthwhile. All the sciences, which did not exist in past eras, are working in this direction. Christian redemption cannot be reduced to historical emancipation and liberation, but at all events it 'remains tied to a critical relationship of solidarity'. Borrowing the title of a bestseller of the 1960s, *Honest to God* – of which the Nijmegen theologian at the time wrote one of the most lucid reviews —, one could describe the characteristics which guide the reflections of Edward Schillebeeckx, whether hermeneutical, christological or theological, as the demand to be 'honest to the world'.

Preface

Since January 1958, the Belgian Dominican Edward Schillebeeckx, the controversial theologian of the Nijmegen School, has been living at the Albertinum or Convent of St Albert the Great. The Albertinum is a grandiose building built at the end of the 1920s and officially opened on 8 September 1932. At one time about one hundred and twenty Dominican brothers were living there, but now there are only about thirty. Between 1942 and 1945 it was occupied by the German army and the brothers went into exile.

At the end of the war, the Albertinum at Nijmegen was again filled with brothers and students. But in the 1980s, when the religious orders were in deep crisis, part of the building was leased to the Catholic University of Nijmegen.

I went there to meet the great theologian Schillebeeckx.

I had been there I don't know how many times to discuss theology with him and to hear what he thought about the burning problems of the present day. I had always been impressed by the massive building, the silence of the convent, the prayer of the brothers, and then those faces of people tossed in the high seas of the tempest. For there was a tempest in the convent, when many were asking to leave because they no longer understood the hidden and celibate religious life or the great building, a structure from a past age, to choose other more intimate places which at the same time were more involved in ordinary life. They have always reminded me of those oaks that stand up to the wind and the rains, which are frequent in the Netherlands and have something mysterious about them. Here were expressions and voices of resistance and courage, with a touch of stubbornness, of Calvinism, an inheritance from the past. Because these people of the Netherlands are not reticent about anything, spare no criticism, have little time for the niceties or for diplomacy. These people are always seeking the light, and reflections are not enough for them; they open the windows to let it all in and illuminate every angle.

Edward Schillebeeckx brought something new to the Netherlands, with a teaching which was increasingly captivating, but which was increasingly regarded with suspicion as time went on, and with ever more mature reflection which at the same time departed further and further from the usual patterns.

In a room overloaded with books – he had his bed behind a curtain – he spoke to me hour after hour about his life: from his happy childhood to the complications over his choice to become a religious; from his study of the humanities, philosophy and theology, to his university teaching at Nijmegen. It has been a courageous life, with the first attacks on his openness coming already at the time when he was working closely with the students of his order. Then there were the phases of his research, the processes in Rome, the nights spent studying scripture and tradition, modern and contermporary authors, in order to answer the questions of people disturbed by the silence of God or fascinated by the gratuitousness of God's presence.

Being face to face with Schillebeeckx, one of the greatest theologians of the century, a prodigy of theological knowledge, does not make you uneasy. He talks as though he had met you on the street and you had asked him for directions; as though he were sitting at a table in a café or by the sea, which fascinates him so much.

I listened to him for days, almost never interrupting him, letting him tell his story and describe his thought, his friendships and the contrasts in his life; I let him talk about his past and his present, with a glance towards the end-time (eschatology), talk about the discovery of a way which shows the greatness of God's mercy in the final encounter with all men and women.

I asked very few questions, just those necessary to remind him that I was playing the part of the man or woman in the street, asking about the God who creates, Jesus of Nazareth who proclaims, the Christ who began the story of a new way of living, a new praxis. And then about the Spirit, which animates a church that always needs to be reformed, for which affection is never enough.

I did not want from Schillebeeckx the theologian a reply to the thousand questions of the man or woman in the street, but rational research, intuition, surprise, even poetry, because Schillebeeckx is also a poet, as is evident from certain pages in the third volume of his christology.

I did not find either bravura or irony in him; far less acrimony about the institutional church, which has often troubled him.

I was looking only for the story of a theologian, who has told us about *Jesus*, *Christ* and *Church* in the three volumes of his christology.

He told me his story, sometimes with a firm voice, at other times in a low voice, being careful about his heart, which has been giving him trouble for some time.

In this account, which was almost dictated, for the most part in French, but sometimes in German and in English, Schillebeeckx has described the riches of his research.

But Schillebeeckx is also involved in the life of the convent, in the festal celebration of the Lord's Day with homilies on various subjects, in the recreation in the late evening, when the brothers, leaving their rooms or returning from the city or the countryside, meet to chat and to joke, drinking wine or beer; or at the extremely frugal meals at which they serve one another.

Theologians and exegetes will still talk for a long time about this man with a boyish face, who does not fit in with the others but whose effervescence, which goes with a penetrating perspicacity, they cannot but forgive.

This is the Schillebeeckx who on that St Dominic's Day 1989, commemorating the foundation of the Order of Preachers, wrote at the beginning of the third volume of his christology: 'I hope that among my readers there will be some of those in authority in the church, who will also listen to the confession of faith of a theologian who all his life did nothing but seek what God can mean for men and women, tentatively and stammeringly.'

This is the Schillebeeckx whom the reader will meet in this account and in the hitherto unpublished writings which follow.

I. The Adventure of a Theologian

I

From Kortenberg to Nijmegen

'I was the sixth of fourteen children in my family: nine boys and five girls. We were never all together, because when my youngest sister was born, my oldest brother was a Jesuit in India. He is still alive. For years he was novice master, and then Father Provincial. At eighty-seven he is still working with the poor. He has also been a professor of dogmatics. He came back from India twice to see our parents. Once he had left for India, it was very difficult to come home. He returned to celebrate our parents' diamond wedding. A request was made to the Father General – at the time a Fleming, Jansen – who told my brother that he had to return to Kortenberg for the celebrations. However, at the time – it was February – they were in the middle of the Ignatian spiritual exercises, which last a month. He indicated that he could not come back to Belgium during February, but only a month later. However, by then my brothers who lived in America had already returned home. So we have no photograph of everyone together. The Jesuit is missing.

I was born on 12 November 1914. It was chance that I was born in Antwerp. My parents lived at Kortenberg, between Brussels and Louvain, but had gone to the Netherlands during the German invasion. At that moment they were in Antwerp on the way home to Kortenberg.

I had a free and very happy childhood because Kortenberg was a close-knit community. The area was a small one and everyone knew everyone else. We numbered about a hundred boys and girls. My parents' educational principle was that we children should be together a lot and educate one another. My father was very strict, but his strictness was quite rational. He discussed, he asked everyone what they thought and accepted different points of view. He was an expert accountant and my mother did the housework. She had a lot of it with fourteen children.

At the age of six I began to serve mass. I liked that a lot. I remember my emotion when the bell rang at the elevation of the host. I thought, "One day I too am going to be a priest." I loved singing. My mother had a very beautiful voice. I remember the Christmases...'

FROM THE JESUITS TO TURNHOUT

'I went to the great Jesuit college at Turnhout at the age of eleven. It was a boarding school. I remained there until I was nineteen. I had to take two preparatory courses because the country schools weren't very good and I hadn't learned enough. I wasn't old enough to study at college. Then I began to study Latin and Greek. Those were eight years of hard study: a programme based purely on the classics, with no courses in English or German.'

'How and why did you become a Dominican when you were nineteen?'

'Here I need to tell the whole story, because I didn't in fact know the Dominicans. I knew only the Redemptorists, who came to hold missions in the country, and of course the Jesuits. Since I had a Jesuit brother, I had intended to become a Jesuit, go to India, and study Hinduism and Buddhism. But I didn't like the discipline in the college. One day, during a period of silence, I was helping a schoolmate with his studies. I had broken the rule of silence. I was severely reprimanded. I defended myself by saying that I had been helping a schoolmate. The reply was, "You must be silent as a matter of principle." Principle!

I felt a deep rebellion inside myself. On the other hand, there was something about the Jesuits of that time which attracted me: their commitment to social questions.

I tried hard to look after the twelve- and thirteen-year-old boys of Turnhout who had no clothes and nothing to eat. There was no instruction for them. They were servants of the college. Father

4

De Wit put me in charge of giving them their catechism lessons. I immediately started a little newspaper for these children. It was a monthly which I produced almost entirely single-handed, with brief articles of a religious, informative, entertaining kind.

At that time, at the age of seventeen or eighteen, I wrote an article for a journal of spirituality edited by Father De Wit which was very concerned with social questions. He aroused my interest in the workers' question. I read many books on the subject. It was the time of Cardijn, the founder of the Jeunes Ouvriers Chrétiens, the time of the great figures in the social field.'

'What subjects did you like best?'

'At that time, before I became a Dominican, I preferred the classics. The Jesuits studied the classical authors, both Latin and Greek, a lot. But the study of the classics was mostly lexical, grammatical, with no grasp of the beauty of the texts. I preferred Greek by far. I came on a lot; I much enjoyed improvising conversations in Greek. I thought that one day I might be a professor of Greek. When I did philosophy with the famous teacher De Petter, who then became a professor at Louvain, I thought of becoming a philosopher. At Ghent, where I did three years of philosophy in the Dominican student house, I fell in love with philosophy.'

'But at this point, let's jump back and hear how you became a Dominican.'

'Towards the end of my studies at the Jesuit college at Turnhout there was a kind of retreat in a Jesuit house. A very austere Jesuit led it. I became convinced that I would never make a Jesuit. Enough of the Jesuits, they were ruining life. I didn't know any other religious order. I wanted to become a religious, a religious priest. I read the lives of St Benedict, St Ignatius, St Francis of Assisi and St Dominic – on Dominic I read *The Spirit of St Dominic*, written by Fr Clérissac. I was struck by the healthy balance, the joy, the openness to the world, the study, the research, the theology centred on preaching. I came to the conclusion that I would become a Dominican. I had once heard a Dominican preaching in a large church and had been impressed: this was Fr van Gestel, who then became my prior at Louvain. He was a sociologist. He didn't have a direct influence on my choice, but when, after reading the life of St Dominic, I decided to become a Dominican, I remembered Gestel's sermon.

I asked myself what I had to do to make contact with the Dominicans. I didn't even know where the convent was. A friend gave me the address of the Dominicans in Ghent. I wrote to the prior, Fr Matthijs, who later became Professor of Metaphysics at the Angelicum. He replied, "Come and visit me in Ghent". It was a lovely letter, which I still keep among my treasures [it is reprinted below, pp. 86–8].

He enclosed a Fra Angelico picture of St Dominic embracing St Francis. I became sure about about my decision to enter the Dominican order. During the vacation in my last year of studying the humanities – I was nineteen – I went to the Dominicans in Ghent and took part in novice life. It was a very hard life. They got up at three in the morning to recite mattins and lauds, an hour of prayer. Then they went back to bed. Terrible! I couldn't have done that all my life because my health was quite fragile. After two days I asked to go. I was then dispensed from getting up in the middle of the night. I felt a bit better. I remember that traumatic experience. After the war the discipline was relaxed.

All in all, I liked that visit to Ghent. I was satisfied.

I finished my studies at the Jesuit college, took the final examinations under three Jesuits who had come from abroad, much known for their classical culture. One of them said to me, "A pity that you're not going to become a Jesuit".

The principal of the college knew that I had written to Ghent because at that time the letters were opened and read. The reply from the prior of Ghent was also known to the superior. He asked me, "Have you written to the Dominicans in Ghent? Do you intend becoming a Dominican?" I replied, "Yes. I've read the life of St Dominic and I would very much like to become a Dominican." He commented, "You're someone who thinks a lot and I'm certain that you've thought it all out. Follow your vocation." I much appreciated his words. The Jesuits remained unhappy about my choice, but didn't put obstacles in the way. I was among the top ones in the class, among the best in the humanities.'

DOMINICAN NOVITIATE IN GHENT

'After the vacation, in September 1934 I entered the novitiate of the Dominican brothers of Ghent. My father went with me and handed me over to the fathers. Life was very hard: the office in the middle of the night, the fast from 14 September, the feast of the Elevation of the Cross, to Easter. In the morning only a piece of bread. At the end of the novitiate I was in pieces. I often fainted. I fell asleep during meditations. At twenty my health was terrible. We were about eight novices in a chapel where it was difficult to breathe. I often fainted in church. I had very severe anaemia. I was dispensed from the fast and recovered.

I began to study philosophy under the guidance of De Petter. Rooted in tradition, his teaching was extremely open to the modern world. At Louvain he had studied phenomenology. He attempted a synthesis between Thomism and the phenomenology of Husserl. He was above all an anthropologist and was able to construct a synthesis between ancient and modern achievements. I was truly taken with his lessons.

I studied philosophy for three years, and before starting theology at Louvain I did a year's military service, during which for some hours during the afternoon we were supervised by clergy, with the possibility of going on theological courses. It was the same for the Protestants and the rabbis. So I received priestly ordination in 1941 after only two years of theology, because the year of theology during military service counted towards ordination.

Then I resumed the study of theology at the Dominican student house in Louvain. These were studies of a classical Thomistic kind.

For two years I was a lecturer in theology, i.e. I taught, in the Dominican study house; after the war, in 1945, I was sent to do my doctorate at Le Saulchoir and in Paris.'

AT SCHOOL WITH THE GREAT THEOLOGIANS

'I met the greats there: Chenu,[1] Congar[2]... Chenu above all had a great influence. He was not a professor at Le Saulchoir at that time because in February 1942 he had been dismissed from his teaching post on the orders of the Holy Office. He was a professor at the École des Hautes Études. I was at Le Saulchoir, near Paris, only on Mondays; the rest of the week I was in Paris and went to the Sorbonne, where great philosophers were teaching: René Le Senne, Louis Lavelle, Jean Wahl. Under the guidance of Chenu I read St Thomas from a historical perspective and not just literally, in the context of the philosophy of the time. At Le Saulchoir I learned to tackle problems from a historical perspective. In my courses, in succession, I went through the Old and New Testaments, the teaching of the Fathers, of St Thomas and the post-Tridentine era. I was convinced that faith and reflection on the faith should be in close contact with the tradition.

I went only to the lectures of the philosopher Étienne Gilson, whose studies of Dante, St Thomas, St Bonaventure and Duns Scotus are among the most important in the field of mediaeval research. These were the people who opened up the historical dimension to me.'

[1] A French Dominican (1895-1990), regent of the faculty of Le Saulchoir from 1920 to 1942, author of *Le Saulchoir. Une École de Théologie* (1937), who was put on the Index in February 1942. He was a *peritus* at Vatican II and wrote a number of books including *Towards a Theology of Work* (1955), *Theology as Event in the Thirteenth Century* (1927) (for more about him see pp. 89–92 below).

[2] A French Dominican born in 1905, a pupil of Chenu at Le Saulchoir, Professor of Fundamental Theology and Ecclesiology there from 1931 to 1954. He was dismissed by the Holy Office, went to Israel, to Jerusalem, and then to Great Britain, to Cambridge. On his return from exile he was welcomed by the Bishop of Strasbourg, where he taught theology at the university until 1958. He was a *peritus* at the Council and is the author of many books on ecclesiology: *True and False Reform of the Church* (1950), *Towards a Theology of the Laity* (1953); and ecumenism – *Diversity and Communion* (1982); *I Believe in the Holy Spirit* (3 vols, 1979-1880).

AT LOUVAIN

'I returned to Louvain in 1947, and in my teaching I remembered my French experience and presented an approach to St Thomas from a historical perspective.

I was responsible for all the courses in dogmatic theology. In four years I taught everything from the theology of creation to eschatology. And I went on doing that for ten years.

I concentrated on studying Holy Scripture by myself. Above all I studied the great Louvain exegete Lucien Cerfaux. I became familiar with the German exegetes, with form criticism[3] and redaction criticism.[4]

Let's go back a bit. After my return from Paris and after I had been teaching for a year, I was appointed spiritual director to the students. I was a professor of all dogmatics, I had so many hours of school, I was confessor in a college, I was spiritual director of about sixty students, for a time confessor to sisters and for six years confessor to prisoners. It was an enormous amount of work. But those were splendid years.

I identified with the students. I got on well with them. At that time the students were quite a different category from the professors and the superiors. Being involved with them, I got to the point of no longer having any contact with the brothers. I lived with the students, ate with them, joked with them. I was convinced of the need to restructure student life. I said that theology has to serve if it is to achieve anything. I was also chief editor of the journal on spiritual life, *Tijdschrift voor Geestelijk Leven*. Now criticisms rained in on me and I had my first major difficulties. There were conflicts with my superiors because I thought their kind of discipline was out of date. Fortunately the Father Provincial protected me. The conservatism was oppressive. I resisted the attacks of the conservatives for more than ten

[3] Form criticism is a method used above all by German exegetes. It is based on the presupposition that the Gospels are formed of small detached units which existed before the Gospels.
[4] Redaction criticism is the method which tries to discover the total conception of each individual redactor (evangelist).

years. I felt that my relations with the students were very important – they were spontaneous, sincere, happy.

In the provincial chapter of the order I suffered a very serious kind of reprimand, so serious that the new provincial, who came from the Congo, where he had taught theology, had to take the case to Rome. There the Master General, Fr Suarez, listened to him. He understood, and told the provincial to suspend the canons against me. He was going against the Constitutions, which state that the canons of a provincial chapter must be observed. The canons remained, but the Master General said that they were to be superseded. The Father Provincial asked me in a very friendly way to take more part in convent life, and I did.'

AT NIJMEGEN IN THE NETHERLANDS

'Professor G.Kreling, who taught dogmatics at the Catholic University of Nijmegen, was near to retirement and was looking for a successor. The Faculty of Theology considered me as a candidate on the suggestion of the famous Professor Grossouw. The Dominican provincial was against this: "We need you as student master." I had trained about 150 students. They still called me "Father Master", or simply "Edward". Then a letter was sent from Nijmegen to the Master General, Fr Brown, a future cardinal, who replied: "When a Dominican has the opportunity to become a university professor, that is where he should be."

I asked the Father Provincial to release me. I went to the provincial and told him that I was ready to go to Nijmegen. "As provincial," he told me, "I am responsible for the province, and it seems to me that you are needed here. So I am opposed to your move. But since for the good of the order you have been called elsewhere, I am happy with it."

I was appointed Professor of Dogmatics and the History of Theology at the Catholic University of Nijmegen in 1957. I came here, to the Albertinum, in January 1958, and after three months began my courses in theology. It was all new to me, including the language. Though Flemish and Dutch are the same language, there are some grammatical differences and differences in pronunciation. It's a bit like English and American.'

'How did you find the new surroundings? I think that you yourself have said that it seemed like returning to the Middle Ages.'

For me this was a new inculturation. After the separation of Belgium from Holland in 1839 the two countries increased their cultural differences and followed their own courses. I had the impression that Holland was more formalistic, more rigid, Calvinistic. But all in all I didn't have very much difficulty getting my bearings.

In those years Catholic theology in the Netherlands was almost non-existent, very poor. I came from Belgium, where philosophy and theology had attained a high academic level. One need only think of the University of Louvain. The University of Nijmegen is quite recent, dating from June 1923.

When I began to teach, the university had only two thousand students, and now it has six thousand. My theology was progressive compared with the theology taught there. I tried not to inculcate a body of doctrine but to analyse history in order to discover the saving action of God and, with this behind me, to return to the present. Theologians have to reflect on their present situation, facing the problems which it raises today, otherwise they are wasting their words. I said this in my courses and seminars. At the time of the student rebellion, every Wednesday I had a course on the most burning questions.

The first thing I did was to start the publication of a new theological journal, *Tijdschrift voor Theologie*, of which I became chief editor: it was a rival to the faculty journal *Studia Catholica*. The first number contained a survey of the new theology: moral, exegetical and dogmatic. It was a programme for the whole faculty. The new review certainly couldn't be said to be the review of the whole faculty, but it was the expression of a completely new way.'

'Have you always had a passion for writing?'

'Yes, as I've told you, while I was still a boy, at the Jesuit college in Turnhout, I began to write, and then as a student I wrote theology and spirituality. I soon published some research studies. For me, writing is second nature. I like it.'

2

The Time of the Council

'At the university of Louvain a historical theology was taught. From the time of Modernism there was a retreat from speculative theology because it was thought to be too dangerous. At that time there was a move towards theological study from a historical point of view and theologians and exegetes of international renown emerged.

In the Netherlands, however, they taught a theology of the manuals. It was my call there which led to my big book *The Sacramental Economy of Salvation*.

It had been my doctoral thesis at Le Saulchoir and was a book of 689 pages, which analysed the sacraments from a historical perspective. The book opened up new horizons, and here at Nijmegen at that time it was much admired. It was a book against sacramental magic, against the *ex opere operato*.[1]

As a young professor at Louvain I set out to review the doctrine of the sacraments from a phenomenological perspective. The whole book was inspired by phenomenology.

At Nijmegen I resumed the courses I had been giving at Louvain. My predecessor, Fr Kreling, a great dogmatic theologian of those times, read St Thomas in an original way, but one which was authentically Thomist, pure scholasticism without the historical dimension. St Thomas was read according to Cajetan, the theologian of the Catholic reform, and the Thomistic theologians of the previous century. In this sense my predecessor opened the way to new developments in reading St Thomas.

When I arrived at Nijmegen, Kreling suggested that I should

---

[1] The sacraments are *per se* efficacious in producing grace.

begin with *De Deo uno*. Instead I began with eschatology.[2] He knew nothing about eschatology. Nothing at all. During all the years of his teaching he had never mentioned it. He was absolutely furious and soon afterwards our relationship came to an end. He was a Dominican, as I was. He lived for another ten years, in increasing isolation, in a little parish run by the Dominicans.

So I began with eschatology, influenced at that time by the studies of the Swiss J.L.Leuba, a Protestant theologian from Neuchâtel, on the history of salvation.

That was the beginning of my reflection on the history of salvation, a concept unknown to the Thomists. It was undoubtedly a very important renewal in the Netherlands. The students who had been taught by Fr Kreling had some difficulties with it at first, but the younger ones were enthusiastic. My theology could no longer be said to be "scholastic"[3] or "neo-scholastic". There was a break between the neo-scholastics and my presence at the university. I found strong support among those in the Netherlands who had at the time had been encouraging the study of psychology and sociology, in a word the human sciences. That was a great change for me. I understood the importance of the human sciences, because the scientific history of the kind that I was pursuing is itself a human science. In that phase of my research the Netherlands gave me a great deal. It was then that a reciprocal influence began between my theology and study of the human sciences, an influence which gave a new dimension to my theological research.

The Dominicans had a review called *De Bazuin* (The Trumpet),

---

[2] *Eschata* is the Greek for extreme, last. Everything relating to the definitive, deepest and ultimate sense of human life is called eschatological. Eschatology deals not only with things after this earth but also with the definitive sense of life, the end-time, in the sense of the time of salvation.

[3] Strictly speaking, mediaeval Christian philosophy. Scholasticism in the first centuries of the Middle Ages was the teaching of the liberal arts and consequently the teaching of philosophy or theology, the first lectures on which were given in the school of the cloister or the cathedral, and then in the university. The scholastic, not trusting in the force of reason alone, appealed to Holy Scripture and tradition. In the nineteenth century the Popes fought for a return to scholasticism (neo-scholasticism) in order to recover the traditions of mediaeval theological and philosophical thought in the framework of modern and contemporary problems.

which was very open, against the preferences of the order. There were conflicts, tensions, but not a break, so that with the passing of time the ideas expressed in *De Bazuin* became the heritage of the greater part of Dutch Catholicism. *De Bazuin* was basic in the preparation for the Council.

But the questions of the time were making themselves felt and called for reflection. The theological faculty also needed serious reform. At that time only people who wanted to get a degree in two years went there. After the Council, others began to come to the faculty who intended to complete all their theological studies there.

At that time, among others, the famous Jesuit dogmatic theologian Piet Schoonenberg was also teaching there.[4] So people began to talk about the "Nijmegen school". The human sciences began to play a part in theological reflection.

Sometimes it is said that Vatican II renewed theology. That is not wholly correct. Vatican II was a kind of confirmation of what theologians like Rahner,[5] Chenu, Congar and others had been doing before the Council.

This amounted to a theological renewal which was no longer overshadowed by neo-scholasticism. Rahner was not a neo-scholastic but a classical author, as in another way was Schoonenberg. Neo-scholastic theology had been abandoned even before the Council.

So the Council was not in fact the starting-point for a new theology, but only the seal on what some other theologians had been doing before the Council; it was the theology of theologians who had been condemned, removed from teaching posts, sent into exile, that triumphed at the Council. So after the Council there was a reaction from Thomist and neo-scholastic theologians who had had no influence at the Council. Already from the end of the Council one could foresee a kind of restoration, because

[4] Dutch, author of *A God of Men* (1969) and *The Adventure of Christology* (1971): a bold reinterpretation of the formula of the Council of Chalcedon on divinity and humanity in Jesus Christ.

[5] A German Jesuit (1904-1984), one of the greatest theologians of the century, whose teaching came under suspicion; however, he was rehabilitated and became a *peritus* at the Council: he wrote a great deal.

there had been no preparation for receiving the renewal of theology. As a result, after the Council a very strong current has developed against these theologians, who have become the targets of suspicions and lies. That is a historical fact.'

REMEMBERING VATICAN II

'Now I can tell you freely and frankly what I think about Vatican II. The Council was a compromise. On the one hand it was a liberal council, which endorsed the new modern values of democracy, tolerance, freedom. All the great ideas of the American and French Revolutions, contested by generations of popes, all the democratic values, were accepted by the Council. On the other hand, the Council could not give a response to the ferments of revolt which were already making themselves felt. That is the irony of history. A council which opened itself to history, to the world, to the society, was soon afterwards overtaken by the new ideas.

The Council didn't tell me anything particularly new. It accepted our theology to some degree, confirming our theological research. We felt free as theologians and liberated from suspicion, from the spirit of the Inquisition and condemnation. The spirit of *Humani generis*[6] (1950), Pius XII's encyclical which condemned Le Saulchoir and La Fourvière, the Dominican and Jesuit schools, had been weighing heavily on us.

All of us had been suspect before the Council, and the Council liberated us. The bishops were in fact open in their pastoral activities, but their theology was old. At that time there was a divide between scholastic theology and pastoral practice.'

---

[6] The encyclical criticized 'the new tendencies which are disturbing the sacred sciences', above all the work of the Nouvelle Théologie, a French theological movement from the period immediately after the Second World War. Theology was to be rethought in the light of the Bible and patristics to meet new philosophical and cultural demands.

FIRST SKIRMISHES

'At the beginning of 1961 a pastoral letter appeared, dated 24 December 1960, signed by all the Dutch bishops. Pope John XXIII had announced the Council. The seven Dutch bishops declared their support for the renewal of the faith and the church. At the end of the document, the episcopate expressed its recognition of those who had worked on it: "We are grateful to Professor E.Schillebeeckx OP of the University of Nijmegen and the Commission for the Apostolate for the valuable service which they have performed in producing the text of this letter." The officials of the Holy Office rightly saw me as the real author of the letter. I had written it from a to z. The letter caused pandemonium, outside the Netherlands as well, and was translated into many languages. From then on the Holy Office began to take an interest in me.'

ROMAN CENTRALISM

'At the first session of the Council (12 October – 9 December 1962), I learned from many contacts with bishops that there was profound resentment against the Roman Curia, even among conservative bishops. The mission bishops above all had a good deal to say. Cardinals Frings of Cologne, Liénart of Lille and König of Vienna openly expressed hostility to the Curia... Many bishops did not want so much a new approach in theology as to break the power of the Curia where it set itself above the bishops. While this was not deliberate, at that time the Holy See nominated as bishops all the secretaries of the conciliar commissions and a large number of members of the Curia. The Curia became even stronger with these names.

At this distance of years I can confirm what the bishops felt about the Curia, that it did not understand what was happening in the church and the world. There was great joy when Pope John, at the request of many bishops, made a change at the Council by rejecting the schema on revelation.

All the Council documents were a compromise. I talked about this with Monsignor Philips of Louvain, the great theologian, a

Belgian senator and a skilful diplomat. He said: "After the Council we shall have many difficulties because of the obscurity of the conciliar documents." That wasn't my view. But after the Council his fears were proved justified. Philips returned to Louvain, and bit by bit the Curia withdrew his powers. Now it seems that it is only Cardinal Ratzinger[7] who is authorized to give an authentic interpretation of the Council. That goes against all the tradition. In this sense I would reaffirm that the spirit of the Council is being betrayed.

Roman centralism, above all in the first session, was on the lips of the bishops, and they could no longer bear it. It was urgent and necessary to break it. With the idea of collegiality, it was thought that the days of centralism were numbered, but on 16 November 1964 there appeared the famous *Nota esplicativa previa*, which explicitly said that the Pope could perform alone some actions for which the bishops were in no way competent, like convening and directing the college, approving the norms for action, and so on. Moreover the supreme pontiff, as the supreme pastor of the church, could exercise his own power at any time at his discretion, as was required by his office.

This was to put a brake on post-conciliar renewal.

What do I recall of this period? Oh yes, the famous opening address of John XXIII on 11 October 1962. What a relief! The Pope said among other things that the substance of the ancient doctrine of the deposit of faith was one thing, and the formulation of it was another.

In the Netherlands, before the Council, some people had got together to propose some questions to send to Rome. For example, there was the restoration of the diaconate. Nothing was said about collegiality, a little on the renewal of matrimony. To tell the truth, there was no great discussion before the Council.

Pope John's address opened up horizons in the Netherlands as well. People began to reassess the Pope, who had lost a good deal

[7] A German, born in 1927, professor of dogmatics, Archbishop of Monaco from 1977-1981, Cardinal in 1977, prefect of the Congregation for the Doctrine of Faith (1981), president of the Biblical Commission and the International Theological Commission.

of prestige with the Synod of Rome (in January 1960), which had been a real farce. There were fears that the Council would meet the same end. The opening address – which was truly prophetic — opened up a great window to the Spirit. People began to think that this would not be the Roman Synod all over again, but something truly new.

The three great innovations of the Council were the contribution of theologians who at one time had been condemned; the anti-curialism of the bishops who came to Rome; and the opening address of John XXIII. These were three factors of the utmost interest, which gave all of us the hope that something was really moving in the church. But to tell the truth, we were not completely certain.

In November 1962, when a decision had to be taken as to whether or not to set the schema on revelation aside, the Pope intervened to get the Council out of an impasse. In fact the opponents of the schema had not secured the necessary two-thirds majority, so they should have gone on considering the schema. John XXIII took the decision to interrupt the discussion, to modify the content of the schema and to entrust this task to a special commission including some cardinals, members of the Theological Commission and members of the Secretariat for Christian Unity. It was a very important decision, a turning point, which had an influence on all the work of the Council. John XXIII made a gesture which would go down in history. He had courage. Cardinal Alfrink[8] was a member of the presidency and told me a good deal of what was going on behind the scenes. There was, for example, the time when he said to me: "Tomorrow morning at nine there will be a sensational announcement: the schema will be remade by a new commission, but please don't pass on the news."

We Dutch used to meet for half an hour each evening to check the situation with the press. Alfrink was very happy. Returning to my room, I heard Bishop Bekkers of 's-Hertogenbosch giving the news to the Dutch press. He was so happy. I said to him,

[8] A Dutch cardinal (1900-1987), famous Archbishop of Utrecht, a member of the Central Commission of the Council, and supporter of *The New Catechism*.

"Excellency, what are you doing?" It was the first time I allowed myself to reproach the bishop of my diocese. He replied to me in astonishment, "Alfrink has asked us to keep quiet, but that doesn't mean that one can't communicate one's joy." Bekkers was like that. But it was the beginning of the break between Alfrink and Bekkers. At the end of the Council the two were no longer on speaking terms. I never understood the real reason for the break. Perhaps it was a kind of love-hate relationship on the part of Alfrink. Certainly Bekkers was ingenuous enough to make some mistakes, but Alfrink – to my regret – never forgave him for his way of doing things. I can understand Alfrink's reaction, but it was exaggerated. When Bekkers, who was ill with cancer, was convalescing in hospital, Alfrink went to visit him and there was a degree of reconciliation. But the fact caused great pain. In the second session no one knew of his illness. Bekkers was no longer himself. He wept often and for no reason. He had terrible headaches.'

ALFRINK AND PAUL VI

'There was a very cordial relationship between Paul VI and Alfrink. Already in the first session of the Council, when Montini was still Archbishop of Milan, Alfrink was invited to give a lecture in Milan, and everyone was aware of the friendship between the two of them. Alfrink certainly had a greater admiration for Paul VI than for John XXIII. They were both abstract intellectuals, but heedful of the problems of the world and the church: extremely sensitive, outwardly calm, almost cold, but inwardly in a ferment. Sometimes Alfrink's intellectualism led him to make some cruel jokes. Like the occasion when he treated Bishop Bekkers badly. Bekkers was a countryman and liked to spend time at the farm among the animals. He was particularly fond of horses. Alfrink went to visit him. I was there too. "They've chosen a very intelligent horse for you," Alfrink said to him with subtle irony. Bekkers understood and took offence beause he was not an intellectual and knew that he was not regarded as one.

I have some criticisms of Alfrink. He was afraid of Paul VI, so afraid that he didn't dare ask him for an audience. At that time there was a need for the two of them to talk about the situation in our Dutch church. I still haven't been able to understand why Alfrink was afraid of Paul VI. Perhaps it was because he came from a small, rigorously Calvinistic country and was himself slightly Calvinistic. The rector of the Dutch College told him, "We need you to go to the Pope and explain our situation to him." And I, too, often said, "Eminence, you must go and talk to the Pope about this or that problem." But he wouldn't agree. He was told to go by Cardinal Ottaviani.[9]

When he finally went for his audience with the Pope he was content. After the Council I was called to Rome to clarify the Catholicity of the University of Nijmegen. I was the president of the university commission and defended the university's choice of openness. The prefect of the Roman Congregation for Catholic Education (the seminaries and study institutes) was Cardinal Garrone.[10] Professor van der Ploeg, a Dominican who lived in Nijmegen but had no relations with the convent, had denounced me to Rome. He had translated into bad French the report of the commission and sent it to Garrone, so I had to go to Rome to clarify the position of the university. In the meantime Alfrink had been summoned to Rome by Šeper,[11] the prefect of the Congregation for the Doctrine of Faith. The issue was the marriage of Professor Grossouw, the great exegete, who had written many books, one of the results of the opening up of the church in the Netherlands. A writer on biblical spirituality, read by thousands and thousand of people, Grossouw had fallen in love and intended to get married. The day of the wedding had already been fixed. Four days before, Alfrink received a telegram from Cardinal Šeper. It called on Grossouw to resign as professor at the University of Nijmegen. Alfrink sent for me and told me about the case. I said to him, "Eminence, all the preparations have been made for

<hr>

[9] Roman cardinal, prefect of the Holy Office, known for his rigidity. He was strenuously opposed to the French Nouvelle Théologie.

[10] Ex-Archbishop of Toulouse, born in 1901. A member of the doctrinal commission at the Council. In 1966 Paul VI nominated him pro-prefect of the Congregation of Seminaries and Studies.

[11] Ex-Archbishop of Zagreb, a key man at Vatican II. He succeeded Cardinal Ottaviani as prefect of the Holy Office.

the wedding." Alfrink didn't say anything to Grossouw. The telegram had explicitly said that the *conditio sine qua non* for the validity of the wedding was that Grossouw should stop teaching. I told Alfrink that Rome could not lay down such a condition for validity since natural law comes before ecclesiastical dispositions. Alfrink held the same view and kept quiet about the situation to Grossouw, who got married in an atmosphere of great devotion and love. I went, and put some flowers in front of the altar of Our Lady. Grossouw knew nothing of the telegram. I told him later.

I met Alfrink in Rome, at the gateway of the Dutch College, on his return for a conversation with Šeper. He was all smiles. He told me about the meeting and passed on Šeper's words, "Eminence, as a pastor I would have done precisely the same." Alfrink was like a boy in difficulites. He lived in a state of constant anxiety.'

'*Do you have any special memories of Paul VI?*'

'At the Dutch National Pastoral Council in 1971 or 1972 the majority were in favour of separating celibacy and priesthood. The Council as such requested Rome to take the option of celibacy into account. It was the beginning of the great contest between the Holy See and Holland, far more so than the famous letter of the Dutch bishops in 1960 on the meaning of the Council. Secretary of State Villot[12] protected Alfrink and told the Pope not to take any action. Alfrink went to the Pope and explained to him the pastoral council's request for optional celibacy. The Pope said: "My view is that celibacy should be optional, but I do not want to go down in history as the Pope who abolished compulsory celibacy." He said that explicitly.

I wrote my book *The Celibacy of the Church's Ministry* in 1965 when I learned from Alfrink what Paul VI had said, with the aim of preparing Dutch Catholics for the separation of priestly ordination and celibacy. That was my intention: to prepare the people for optional celibacy. The most progressive people attacked me because the book was not strong enough. I was convinced –

---

[12] Ex-Archbishop of Lyons, one of the five deputy secretaries at the Council. He was called to Rome by Paul VI.

as I still am over other questions – that if people are not prepared, a great mistake is being made, and that it is bad to introduce innovations which cause damage rather than helping the life of the church to progress. For example, there is the ordination of women. People have to be informed, instructed, involved in the question, otherwise things go wrong. Alfrink was completely in accord with me over the book on celibacy.'

AN AUDIENCE WITH PAUL VI

'Before the Council ended, Alfrink asked the Pope for an audience for me. He told him that he had twice asked that I should be appointed an official *peritus* at the Council, to no avail. Paul VI told Alfrink that he would like to see me. He didn't know that Cardinal Ottaviani had always been opposed to my nomination as an official *peritus*. I was told to go for my audience with the Pope. That was on 4 December 1965.We talked for a little more than half an hour. I hardly managed to say anything to him. I tried to talk to him but he kept interrupting me suddenly and brusquely. He spoke perfect French. I wanted to say something but he would not let me. It was a painful business. Later I told Alfrink that the audience had been a disappointment. The Pope told me, "I am truly content with what you said in your lectures at Domus Mariae on the eucharist." At that time I was defending transignification. The encyclical *Mysterium fidei* had just come out (this was September 1965), and I began my lecture by praising the encyclical. I said that I was against transignification understood as pure symbolism and that transubstantiation[13] is a transignification

[13] 'Transubstantiation' is the transformation or conversion of the bread into the body and the wine into the blood. 'Transignification' is the transformation or conversion of the bread into the body and the wine into the blood. Transignification is a radical transformation of the ultimate meaning of what the bread is after consecration. Before consecration the bread is nutrition for the body, whereas after consecration the bread is totally spiritual nutrition.

'Transfinalization': the bread is bodily nutrition, but the aim of the consecrated bread is a spiritual nutrition, a gift of Christ the saviour.

'Transignification' and 'transfinalization' are concepts nearer to the

in an ontological sense.[14] The Pope told me: "They're reported that you've become one of us." I didn't understand what he meant. I had the sensation of not having been clear. Why should I have become "one of us"? I am one of the church. Who are these "us"? I certainly had observations to make on the encyclical, but I expressed them blandly. I had observations on transignification as pure symbolism. For me transignification was ontological, something quite different from a physical transignification. Someone tried to explain the expression used by Paul VI as meaning that the Pope was not opposed to my ideas on the eucharist.

However, I didn't think this a very happy expression.

He encouraged me to continue my research, expressed himself content with the lectures. I wanted to defend myself by saying something about my theology, but he wouldn't let me. At the end of the audience he took out a rosary from a drawer and said, "Take it to your father." And what about my mother? He gave me another one. Then he called the secretary, who brought in the photographer. That was the end of the audience.

At the door I met the Benedictine abbot Basil Hume, who was to become Archbishop of Westminster. He said to me, "Fr Schillebeeckx, keep going on as you are".'

THE CONCILIAR DOCUMENTS: A COMPROMISE

'Let me repeat something which I have already said in part: the Council affirmed those liberal, modern values which the church had contested in the past. The Council adopted these values: a respect for freedom of conscience, of religion, tolerance. These are modern values as such, which the church had combatted up to Pius XII. The Council accepted all this. In this sense it was a

---

modern mentality. With these new terms Schillebeeckx seeks to give better expression to the anthropological significance of the eucharistic presence in relation to that of the believer and the church.

The ultimate destination of the bread changes profoundly with consecration.

[14] After the consecration the 'reality' of the bread is something different, specifically the body of Christ.

council which adopted some values of the modern world. It can be defined as a modern liberal council. Certainly it did not criticize society, as the student movements of 1968 were then to do. It is true that the conciliar constitution *Gaudium et spes* (The Church in the Modern World) of 7 December 1965 was a little too optimistic, but it was right, because it began from the principle that the Holy Spirit is in action everywhere. In truth the 1960s were full of hope. After that would come the challenge to society. It is a kind of irony that on the one hand the Council adopted liberal values, and on the other it was suddenly overtaken by the critical movements of modern society. So it was a modern council in the sense that it accepted modern values, but at a time when postmodernity was already making itself felt. The crisis of liberal values was already beginning, and the demands of solidarity were making themselves felt. Reflection on the church of the poor was already under way, but this was not to dominate the conciliar texts. The various messages at the end of the Council (December 1965) suggest that it was already going down another road. However, the conciliar texts are the fruit of compromises. Gutierrez[15] himself, the father of liberation theology, told me that he had been inspired to begin his theology more by the conciliar messages than by the texts themselves.'

THE NETHERLANDS IN THE COUNCIL

'You ask me if I remember the controversial Dutch Pastoral Council, which some people called a synod. Monsignor de Vet, Bishop of Breda, had the idea that it would be possible to hold a kind of council in the Netherlands to take up all the themes of Vatican II. Cardinal Alfrink agreed. I encouraged him to do so. After some time preparations began for the pastoral council. About a dozen commissions were formed. The criticism directed at the pastoral council was that it was a council made up of intellectuals, university professors, scientists, educated and

[15] A Peruvian theologian, author of *A Theology of Liberation*, the first systematic treatment of this theology. He has written much on the situation in Latin America.

important people involved at the upper level of church movements, society people and entrepreneurial. The preparations for the council were very serious and very detailed. There were many meetings and assemblies, and finally the twelve commissions presented their reports. Obviously they were very open. This was a new *aggiornamento* of Vatican II. Every commission referred to Vatican II, but went much further in all fields. For example, the commission on faith went well beyond Vatican II. So did the commission on ministry. All the great theologians were there: dogmatic, exegetical, moral theologians. It was a synod, but since the word 'synod' frightened people, we called it the Pastoral Council of the Netherlands.

Rome didn't look kindly on it from the beginning because there was no distinction between hierarchy and the laity. In Belgium after the Council there was a kind of pastoral council, but it didn't overdo things in that respect and Rome was satisfied. The Netherlands is not a land of compromises.

The council was a great success. Every session lasted several weeks and the various reports were discussed up until 1972. Things were increasingly moving towards an openness which bothered Rome. Problems of ministry continually emerged, and therefore the problem of celibacy. There were conservatives in the council, but only a few, who continually attacked the council's reports very harshly. They went so far as to denounce various people to Rome and thus increased the mistrust of the Holy See.

It is true that within the pastoral council attacks were launched by ordinary people; by workers, for example, only three or four of whom were present. They openly showed their unease and this made a great impression. It is true that in the Netherlands the working class was not taken into consideration; the situation is not like that in Belgium, where the working class is very strong within the church, even if many workers abandoned it at the time of industrialization. The Walloons detached themselves from the church, but the French speakers did not do so to the same extent. In the Netherlands, however, the working class did not abandon the church and was not taken account of in the pastoral council, where it carried no weight. The ordinary person wasn't represented. We made a mistake there. There were two open meetings at which workers, students, young people and all kinds of others took part and could speak freely.

There were moving testimonies which were very effective. The commissions were integrated with other elements. We were so much daggers drawn with Rome that in 1972 the council[16] closed, with some satisfaction, because despite the opposition of Rome it was felt that people were together, now that we had listened to the men and women in the street.

The council adopted the reports and these continued to be studied and discussed in the parishes and to be deepened.The conclusions did not have the approval of the Holy See, but this was not thought to be particularly important.'

THE HOLY SEE AND THE STORM OVER THE NETHERLANDS: *THE NEW CATECHISM*

'There was the question of the catechism. Rome insisted on corrections, but Alfrink defended it. In the Netherlands no account was taken of the supplement with the corrections, it was not even put on sale.'

At this point we break off the conversation and insert a section on The New Catechism, *over which there was so much discussion*

It was on 1 March 1966 that Archbishop Cardinal Bernard Alfrink gave the *imprimatur* at Utrecht to *The New Catechism – A Proclamation of Faith for Adults*. The bishops wrote in the intoduction: 'The term "new" should not be misunderstood. This does not mean that modifications have been made to some points of the faith while all the others remain unchanged. Had that been so, we could have contented ourselves with changing some pages of the old catechism. That has not happened. On the contrary,

---

[16] In fact the Dutch Pastoral Council went on after 1972. After the conclusion of the third assembly on 6 January 1984 it was forced to modify its statutes. From then on it was convened by the bishops and followed an agenda laid down by the hierarchy.

the whole of the message, the whole of the faith, has remained identical, but the way of approaching it, of illuminating it, is new. Any living being must at the same time both remain the same and be renewed. The message of Christ is a living message. Thus *The New Catechism* seeks to announce the eternal faith in a form suited to our times.'

The book, more than six years' work, was without doubt unique. Its fascinating style and modern language drew the attention to it of people not only in the Netherlands but also abroad, provoking on the one hand a wave of enthusiasm and on the other anxieties and requests for precision. So much so that the Holy See could not remain silent. There was a meeting between three theologians nominated by Rome and three theologians chosen by the Dutch episcopate. They discussed from 8 to 10 April 1967. The Vatican side asked for some 'well thought out precisions' to be introduced into the catechism. The Dutch said no. Paul VI wanted changes to be made, for example over the virginal conception of Jesus Christ, the doctrine of the existence of angels and the sacrificial character of the redemption of Christ. A commission of cardinals (Frings of Cologne, Lefebvre of Bourges, Jaeger of Paderborn, Florit of Florence, Brown of the Roman Curia and the Swiss Journet) were charged with the task of examining the text.

The cardinals met on 27 and 28 June 1967, along with theologians who knew Dutch. They decided that before the publication of new editions and translations, *The New Catechism* had to be 'diligently revised and corrected'.

A second theological commission was formed, drawn from seven nations, which was entrusted with the task of examining the text and expressing a view. The cardinals, taking note of the observations of the theologians, met on 12-14 December 1956, noted the modifications which had to be introduced, and gave instructions that this was to be done by a small commission composed of two theologians from the Dutch episcopate and two chosen by the commission of cardinals. These finished work in February 1968 and submitted the results to the Holy See, the commission of cardinals and the Dutch episcopate.

In the meantime *The New Catechism* had been published without the approval of the Dutch episcopate and without any corrections, first in English and then in German and French. The Italian edition with the 'Declaration of the Commission of Cardinals' and the 'Supplement to *The New Catechism*' was given the *imprimatur* by the Archbishop of Turin, Cardinal Michele Pellegrino, on 31 May 1969.

We return to Schillebeeckx, who makes this comment:

'First of all it should be noted that the catechism was conceived and written before Vatican II. It was published afterwards, in 1966, but the basic ideas are preconciliar. So these are not the innovations made by the Council. At that time, when the discussions were quite advanced, I was asked by Cardinal Alfrink to look at the text carefully, an admirable work by a team of Jesuits at Nijmegen headed by Fr van Hemert. I read it all and asked for a change to one formula, which was repeated about twenty times, namely that Jesus is a human person, giving the impression that he is not God.

The correction was accepted. That was my only contribution. Granted, this was a preconciliar catechism, but I found it too individualistic. It lacked a political and social dimension. It is too pious a text. By this I don't mean to detract from its beauty, which shines through everywhere. It is a book of its time, and arises out of the atmosphere of the 1960s.'

THE NETHERLANDS DIVIDED: THE NEW BISHOPS

'The pastoral council was beyond doubt a great event for the Netherlands. It went beyond Vatican II and provoked reaction. For example, Monsignor Simonis opposed it with all his might. Still a student at Rome at the time of the Council, he was against Vatican II and the Dutch bishops. After Vatican II, in the Netherlands there were to be some nominations of bishops opposed to conciliar openness. Simonis and Gijsen were nominated bishops of Rotterdam and Roermond respectively, at the time of the storm over the pastoral council, to combat all new ideas and break up the internal unity of the conference of bishops. They argued for restoration and took every possible opportunity of openly criticizing the pastoral council. Little by little, under pressure for Rome, other bishops fell silent, but in the parishes things went on as before. The break with Rome became increasingly marked. Priests and faithful no longer understood their bishops and increasingly parted company with them. So there was not only friction with Rome but above all disunion within the Dutch church. That was the drama of those days.

The people did not suffer much over the difficulties with Rome, but they suffered and are still suffering a good deal as a result of the frictions within the church community. There continues to be no dialogue between the bishops and the faithful. It is a disaster brought about by questionable nominations.

I am not against the conservative bishops, but bishops have been nominated[17] who do not have the understanding needed to grasp history. They can be conservative, but they must be intelligent conservatives at a pastoral level. Before he became a bishop, Simonis was a splendid pastor, but now as a bishop it is not pastoral work which counts but the principle, obedience to Rome. In a way he is unintelligent. Some bishops say incredible things about the faith, Jesus Christ, sexuality, women.

Many intellectuals, at one time leaders of movements, have left the church. This is a loss which lies very heavy on church life. Many have become indifferent. The church is no longer of interest. The result of these nominations is a profound sadness everywhere. This is certainly not a normal situation. The struggle continues between the parish priests and their bishops. There is tension in some parishes: for Rome and against Rome; for Simonis and against Simonis; for Gijsen and against Gijsen; for Bomers and against Bomers. For Dutch Catholics Rome, the Holy See, is the Roman Curia, bureaucratic and oppressive. Before the Council the Dutch Catholics were closely bound to Rome and the Pope; now everything has been turned upside down. There has been a

[17] In 1982 four auxiliary bishops were nominated: de Kok and Nieuhaus in Utrecht, Casterman in Roermond, Bär in Rotterdam. In 1983 Simonis went to Utrecht and Bomers was nominated to Haarlem. In 1985 Ter Schure succeeded Bluyssen at 's-Hertogenbosch. Many Catholics, priests and laity, were affected and attacked the Holy See for the authoritarian exercise of its power.

move from preconciliar papalism to attacks, indifference, silence. It is a sad and abnormal situation.'

3

The Processes

THE FIRST PROCESS ON SOME THEOLOGICAL ESSAYS (1968)

'I had no idea that a process was being prepared against me. Rahner told me. He had asked if he could pay me a visit, "but not in the convent because one of your Dominican brothers has denounced you to Rome". This was Professor van der Ploeg, who taught exegesis at the University of Nijmegen. He founded two very conservative journals in which he attacked bishops and theologians. Rahner told me that the question was so delicate that he could not talk to me on the telephone. I invited him to the secretariat of the journal *Concilium* at Nijmegen. Rahner had been designated *relator pro auctore* (advocate) with the task of defending me against the attacks and suspicions. He sent me a dossier with all the denunciations of me by my Dominican brothers and the pro-nuncio. I read it at a sitting. However, it was only interviews given to newspapers and magazines in America.

The first process was about my ideas on secularization. My thought was this: the human fields are autonomous as such. Rahner took back the dossier in the future, promising me that he would send it back one day, but his death prevented him from ever giving it to me. So it's in Innsbruck, in the Rahner archive.

He was the only one to know that there was a process against me. Secrecy had been imposed on Rahner on pain of grave sin, but he told me that natural law came before an objective disposition. I didn't talk with anyone. After two or three months – I had been in America giving some lectures – I told my secretary, the Dominican Fr Truyman, an expert on the mass media. He asked me: "Can I mention it to Fesquet, the religious correspondent of

Le Monde? Can I ask him to investigate in Rome whether it is true that there are proceedings against you?" Everything was secret. In 1942 Fr Chenu had learned that he had been condemned from the radio. Three months later, Truyman went to Paris to talk with Fesquet, who promised that he wouldn't publish the news before a rigorous investigation.

A year later, Truyman reported that Fesquet had gathered all the information. On 24 September the news appeared in the French newspaper *Le Monde*.[1]

But who had talked without taking account of the secrecy on pain of grave sin? Who had let out the secret? The Holy Office was absolutely furious, while the church world took a stand against the inquisitorial procedures of Rome. Rahner was suddenly summoned to Rome. It was thought that he was the one who had talked. It was impossible that it could have been the members of the Holy Office. The secretary of the Roman congregation at that time was Monsignor Philippe, a Dominican. Rahner subsequently told me that he had been interrogated by Philippe for three hours. "I said nothing to Schillebeeckx", the great German theologian continue to repeat to Philippe, who ultimately gave in and apologized to Rahner.

It was indeed Rahner who told me that I was being investigated, and that he felt it his moral duty to tell me. For him it was a real injustice to behave like that. As an advocate, he had to speak with his client. The secrecy was part of church law, and natural law came before that. "This time my conscience told me to make a mental qualification",[2] Rahner repeated to me.

Rahner's assistant, the German theologian Lehmann, wrote the

---

[1] 'The tremors caused by the encyclical *Humanae vitae* are far from dying down. We have now learned that the Congregation for the Doctrine of the Faith, unknown to the party concerned, has begun a kind of process on the suspicion of heresy against Fr E.Schillebeeckx, in whom for many years Cardinal Alfrink has put his trust. Schillebeeckx is known as the theologian of the Dutch episcopate' (*Le Monde*, 24 September 1968).

[2] 'Mental qualification' is an internal act of the mind by which while one is speaking one utters the words with a meaning which is not their obvious one.

Because it is legitimate to argue that to conceal the truth is a duty or at least very useful and this is the only means available.

text for the defence. Rahner made his assistants work very hard. He asked Lehmann to read all my publications and write the defence.

On Monday 7 October 1968 Rahner spoke before the consultants to the Congregation – perhaps nineteen of them – and all had to give their evaluation of my writings. I knew that the theologian Daneels, who later became Bishop of Antwerp and is now Archbishop of Malines-Brussels, was not present: he was very open. I believe that he was not even invited. Only theologians of the Roman school were present.

Rahner spoke after the statement by the consultants to the congregation. He criticized the method adopted and denounced the lack of trust in theologians who were guilty only of not using the ordinary vocabulary. He spoke with passion.

His exposition made an enormous impression. No decision was taken that day. The result was communicated to the plenary assembly of the cardinals of the Congregation, who in their turn made a report to the Pope. Neither Rahner nor I were informed of the results of the vote.

Rahner telephoned me two hours after the conclusion of the debate and told me that many of the consultants to the Congregation were in agreement with my ideas, perhaps two-thirds.

On 15 January 1971 Jerome Hamer, the prefect of the Congregation for the Doctrine of Faith announced, new rules for the procedure in processes. In fact at my second process in 1979 everything followed the new procedure. But now, with Ratzinger, these rules are not respected because he has informal conversations with the theologian under investigation. There is no formal procedure. It seems to me that this is much worse. Everything is up to him, while Hamer's norms contained very precise directions. These norms can be criticized, but the person under investigation can defend himself in a serious and orderly way.'

THE SECOND PROCESS ON CHRISTOLOGY (1979)

'There was another secret investigation by the Congregation for the Doctrine of Faith into my christology *Jesus*, published in

1974. A questionnaire was drawn up which was sent to me on 20 October 1976.

The introduction said that there were numerous statements in my work which caused serious perplexity, about methodological principles, the results of exegetical research, and dogmatic theology. I was asked to clarify my thought:

1. On the preference given to certain exegetical trends and the use of hermeneutics;

2. On the historical Jesus with reference to his human person, his prophetic-eschatological mission, his relationship to the Father and finally his resurrection;

3. On the mysteries of the Incarnation and the Trinity; on the virginal conception of Jesus and the church.

On 13 April 1977 I sent a detailed reply, in writing and in French, to all the questions put to me by the Congregation.

On 18 July I received a second questionnaire from the Congregation. Some questions could be said to have been clarified and resolved, but some other points of doctrine remained suspect. I understood that I was involved in another process on questions different from those sent to me in October 1976.

Through Cardinal Willebrands,[3] Archbishop of Utrecht, on 6 July 1978 I was asked to go to Rome to explain my position on the new christological questions.

In December 1979 I went to Rome to appear before three theologians under the presidency of the prefect of the Congregation. On 13 December Hamer read an introductory text which stated that the Congregation would keep to the rules laid down on 15 January 1971; then there was a reminder of the questionnaire sent to me on 20 October 1976 and my reply which arrived on 26 April 1977. Hamer remarked that the colloquium, as provided for by the rules, was taking place in an "ecclesial spirit of respect and mutual trust".

The prefect could be represented by the secretary, and so Monsignor Bovone was to preside over the colloquium. There

[3] Dutch, born in 1909, made cardinal in 1969, Archbishop of Utrecht from 1975 to 1983, president emeritus of the Pontifical Council for the Promotion of Unity among Christians, a chamberlain of the College of Cardinals. He is one of the leading figures in the Catholic church.

were present: the great Louvain exegete, A.Descamps, whom I knew well; the Dominican A.Patfoort, Professor at the Angelicum; and J.Galot, a Jesuit from the Gregoriana. Patfoort was a Fleming from Lille, who knew a little about my books on the sacraments, but not the other publications. He had difficulties, the poor thing! Galot brought out the interviews I had given before the summons to Rome. I retorted by saying that my thought is in books and not in interviews, which are always incomplete. Then he brought out the text and photograph of the celebration of the marriage of a priest in a Dutch parish, in which I was giving the address. I firmly said to Galot that this had nothing to do with the process.

At one point Bovone intervened: "Schillebeeckx is right. We need to discuss his work." But Galot wouldn't give in and Bovone had to shut him up. Galot took it badly. He was furious.

Each of the three theologians had half an hour to talk. Patfoort caused me trouble. He asked me questions which were out of place and ingenuous. He asked me to explain hermeneutics to him. I replied with a slogan from St Thomas (he was an observant Thomist): *Quidquid recipitur, ad modum recipientis, recipitur* (whatever is received is received in a way suited to the recipient). "Ah, now I understand," he said. "Fine, fine." That was that.

Descamps knew me well. He had often invited me to lecture at Louvain, even at retreats for priests. He made some remarks from an exegetical perspective: "I am here as an exegete and not as a dogmatic theologian." With much competence and courtesy he had reviewed my book in the Louvain theological journal (in 1975) and I took account of his criticisms.

At the colloquium, while restating the criticisms, he praised my research.

The process revolved round my book *Jesus*, though in the meantime a second volume, *Christ*, had been published.

The colloquium process lasted for two and a half days. The theologians read their prepared statement while I had to reply off the cuff to all kinds of questions. In fact I was facing a new process because I had already replied to the first questionnaire in writing in 1977. An attempt was being made to unseat me. I was not condemned. Some questions remained in suspense. So the process turned out well for me.

On 20 November 1980 I received a letter from the Congregation inviting me to clarify some points and to remove some ambiguities. There was no condemnation in the letter. Some questions remain open on matters which are not in accord with the doctrine of the church, but they are in accord with the faith. That is very important.'

THE THIRD PROCESS ON THE MINISTRY (1984)

'The third process was about my book *Ministry* (1980). The process was begun under Hamer, whom I knew well because we were together at Louvain, but was conducted and concluded by Ratzinger, who had become prefect of the Congregation in November 1981.

In the meantime, in September 1982, I had stopped teaching at the University of Nijmegen, so I was not there under the Grand Chancellor of the University, Cardinal Simonis, Archbishop of Utrecht.

The Master General of the order, Vincent de Couesnongle, received a dossier about me which was then sent to me by the Father Provincial. There was a request to form a commission of Dutch theologians to examine my book. This was formed. They unanimously stated that there was nothing in it against the faith, that in fact theologically speaking the presence of the extraordinary ministry exists in almost all the sacraments and is recognized by the official doctrine of the church. I argued that in some extraordinary circumstances recourse could be had to the presidency of an extraordinary ministry.

Ratzinger received the report from the commission of Dutch theologians. On 6 August 1983 he published the letter on the priestly ministry in which he argued that the exclusion of an extraodinary ministry for the eucharist had been decreed by the Fourth Lateran Council. Ratzinger forced the council text and drew a logical conclusion because the council said that only ordained priests could preside at the eucharistic celebration, since at this time there were deacons who presided at it. There were many cases in the East. When the bishop could not be present, the deacon presided as a representative of the bishop. Ratzinger said that the matter was closed.

Two or three months after the publication of the letter Ratzinger himself told me that the matter was closed and that there was no place for the extraordinary minister in presiding over the eucharist. The last word had been spoken, but it was the word of Ratzinger. Certainly the Pope has given his consent, but this is not a papal act. I do not understand how the matter can be closed. It's surprising. I've written an epilogue to the French edition of my book on ministry in which I criticize Ratzinger for taking upon himself the right to interpret a council, Lateran IV, in his own way.

After the publication of Ratzinger's document I wrote a new book on ministry. I no longer talked of extraordinary ministry, but asked for a kind of sacrament for pastoral workers, who could thus receive an ordination in the context of the sacramental ministries. So I no longer speak of an extraordinary ministry of presiding over the eucharist, but use another category to refer to the same thing.

The Master General told me to go to Rome for a colloquium with Ratzinger. Ratzinger's secretary was also there, and we talked in English, which Ratzinger speaks well. The colloquium lasted about three quarters of an hour and was very cordial. This was not a process in accordance with the 1971 norms, but a simple colloquium, quite informal. It is a worse procedure than a regular process. I met Ratzinger face to face and recalled the times of the Council. Already then there was something about him which didn't convince me. He never spoke in the meetings during the Council. Rahner, Chenu and Congar were there and he did not speak.

During our conversation he was very kind. I told him that in the new book I no longer spoke of the extraordinary ministry. I was simply asking for a new ordination with the epiclesis.[4] He asked me what I was doing now that I had stopped teaching at the university. I replied that I was working harder than ever. He continued to ask me questions. For me this form of colloquium

---

[4] The prayer in the mass with which, especially in the Eastern liturgies, the Holy Spirit is called down on the sacrificial offerings so that they become the body and blood of Christ and thus the means of salvation for those who take part in the eucharist.

can work well because I am of a certain age, but for younger people it's a gentle form of torture. They can't know what lies behind his kindness and affability.

I went out accompanied by the secretary. The Master General indicated that he had something to say on the colloquium, but the secretary interrupted him, saying: "Perhaps this will be the new procedure of the Congregation: a colloquium between Ratzinger and the theologian." The Master General and I kept quiet. Then in the *Osservatore Romano* a note appeared for the Christian people in which it was said that for the Congregation there were still some points of disagreement with the official doctrine of the church, but not with the faith.

In short, I was never condemned in the three processes.'

'Did these processes cause you a lot of suffering?'

'I wouldn't say a lot. In the first, when Rahner told me that I was being investigated without my knowing why, I remained terrified. I remember saying to Rahner: "To think that this treatment is reserved for those of us who have worked day nad night for the church." In the second process I was bothered a bit, but I felt freer towards the Roman Congregation, the theological inquisitors and myself. It was an open process and I felt at ease, despite the presence of Galot, which disturbed me. I asked myself how all this could be possible in the church of God. As theologians we are not infallible, but there is a right way and a wrong way to treat people.'

'Has it ever occurred to you to leave the church and the order, as the Brazilian theologian Leonardo Boff[5] has recently done?'

'Never, never. I belong to the Roman Catholic church, but I wouldn't want say that this church can't make mistakes. In fact one needs to have the courage to say so. And then to leave the

[5] A key exponent of liberation theology, the author of numerous highly successful works. He left the priesthood and the Franciscan order on 27 June 1992.

Dominican order? I've never doubted the choice I made at the age of nineteen. I feel sorry about Boff's choice. He is a very dear friend, committed to the poor, but what he has done disconcerts me. I'm very sad.

To end this chapter on the processes, I would say that up to now, as I hope will always be the case, I have never had any kind of condemnation, and despite the adventures, I am happy to belong to this church and to the Dominican order.'

4

Theological Research

'There has been evolution in my theological reflection. I began by commenting on what you might call *sacra doctrina* in St Thomas. It is not the sacred doctrine of the church, but Holy Scripture, which includes not only the Bible but also patristics and the whole Christian tradition. There are two currents in St Thomas: one accepts the use of sacred doctrine with reference to theology, the other argues that theology begins with the Bible and that the Bible is the foundation of all theology. Theology is the Bible, which expands in history. In the first phase of my theological reflection I followed the method of sacred doctrine.

In the 1960s, along with the arrival of the human sciences, there appeared criticism of society, of culture, of ideology and also of theology as a theological discipline. I followed this trend. So I entered a hermeneutical phase, which in fact developed side by side with the critical phase. I faced the problem of the interpretation of texts because hermeneutics as such was hardly known, either in Catholic or in Protestant circles. People talked instead of the evolution of dogmas. First I talked of the evolution of dogmas, then of the evolution of the Christian tradition and then, in the 1960s, of hermeneutics.[1]

I then tackled the trend towards structuralism.[2]

[1] Hermeneusis is 'interpretation' and 'hermeneutics' is the 'science of interpretation' which investigates the presuppositions of hermeneusis or interpretation (for example, of the Bible). This investigation is necessary because of the progressive broadening of the horizon of our experiences, our reflection and our way of expressing such experiences.

[2] The term 'structuralism' relates to very different linguistic schools which have in common the fact that they base linguistics on the study of what has been said, trying to define its structure (architecture, independence of internal elements), while everything relating to its enunciation (i.e. the subject and the situation) is left outside research.

For me hermeneutics is not just the hermeneutical or interpretative problem: it is the science of interpretation which investigates the presuppositions of an interpretation. In the first chapter of the third volume of my christology I outline a synthesis of the cognitive structure of human experience. I speak of an experience of faith in the Bible not understood as a theology of the word because the word of God is the word of human beings who speak of God. To say just like that that the Bible is the word of God is simply not true. It is only indirectly the word of God. The biblical writings are human testimonies to God, by people who have lived a history and experienced God. When the Bible says, "God has said it, Christ has said it...", it is not God or Christ who has said it in the strict sense, but human beings who have told of their experience of God. Their experience comes from the Spirit, and in this sense it can rightly be said that the Bible is inspired.

However, at the same time we need to remember the human, historical, contingent mediation. Human beings never have a direct encounter with God, face to face; this encounter always takes place through intermediaries. It is human beings who talk of God.

This is very important for theological research and for understanding the evolution of dogmas. The new theology cannot be understood without this concept of revelation mediated by history, of the interpretative experience of human beings. When the mediation is not accepted, one inevitably slips into fundamentalism.

My theological method is based on human and Christian experience, communal and personal. I apply it to tradition, which is an experience that becomes extended. Individuality is included in this communal experience. In my theological reflection I continue to apply the method of experience.'

CONFRONTING MODERNITY

'I have analysed modernity from Nicholas of Cusa to Descartes, Leibniz and Pascal. One year I gave a course on Marx, a product of modernity on the one hand and a critic of the subjectivity which lies at the core of modernity on the other.

I now see that there is a tendency to oppose modernity, regarding it as a kind of Antichrist. The present Pope seems to be denying modernity with his project of the re-evangelization of Europe. The Pope says that there is a need to return to the old Europe of Cyril and Methodius and of St Benedict. For John Paul II, the return to the Catholicism of the first millennium is the great challenge. Then follow the centuries of schism, first with the East and then within Western Christianity. In the second millennium Europe declined, and with it the whole of Western culture. To re-evangelize Europe there is a need to overcome modernity and all the modern values and go back to the first millennium. To return to rural Christianity, the model of all Christianity. If that is so – I would add – there is also a need to have the courage to accept the theology of ministry in the first millennium. But this Pope says nothing about that. Premodern, agricultural, uncritical Christianity is the model of Christianity in the Pope's thought: "France, what have I done for your baptism?" That is the typical expression of this return. I criticize this return because the modern values of freedom of conscience, tolerance and religion are not in fact the values of the first millennium.'

'At one point you spoke of secularization. I was interested in this. Do you think this term is outdated?'

For me secularization is increasingly a concept which is not properly understood. I understand secularization as a historical and cultural phenomenon in which the world and society are planned within a rational cognitive horizon. Human beings plan the world and work with a view to a future, and in this way a source disappears from which religion was in fact nourished in the past. I understand secularization in the sense of terrestrial autonomy. The bishops and Rome see secularization as the cause of all evils. They blame secularization for having dulled the religious sense, and so on. Clearly secularism has done that, but it is quite a different phenomenon from secularization.

So I prefer to talk of modernity, of postmodernity, even if this is an inflated and ambivalent term. There is a postmodernity in present conditions, in which human beings are a structure.'

'There is a distinction between the project which I have always had in my head and my occasional works. At the University of Nijmegen I didn't have to give fixed courses, but only to deal with questions. I could choose the subjects myself. Towards the end of the 1960s, the time of the great conflicts, the students forced me to compromise: to maintain my course and deal with some topical subjects. At Louvain I had to give compulsory courses; at Nijmegen I could choose. I centred my reflection on eschatology and christology. But on the other hand, cirucmstances led me to tackle specific themes which were occasioned by particular situations. In the theological journals (*Concilium, Tijdschrift voor Theologie*...) I published articles which related to facts in the church and the world. In a certain sense, on the one hand I did a contextual theology and on the other I continued my project. The three volumes of christology were also occasioned by the crisis in christology throughout theology, whether Protestant or Catholic. It was a personal project, which has always enthused me. In most recent years I have begun to discuss creation in relation to eschatology. This is research which continues.

However, the books on ministry were prompted by the pastoral situation in the Netherlands and as reflected in the Catholic world.

To sum up, on the one hand some writings are contextual, prompted by events and problems, whether in the world or in the church, and on the other there are works which arose from my personal project. Above all the works on christology.

II. Points of Research

5

Creation

'Now I intend to look at some specific themes of my research to which I attach great importance. This is the first time that I have frankly expressed my thoughts on some of these topics, since I am aware that I may cause some perplexity. They are topics which I have been studying day and night because they interest me a great deal.

I begin with creation.

I regard the creation as the foundation of all theology. At present there is a kind of appeal from many sides for theology to restore the treatment of creation to its true place. There is so much talk of the history of salvation that there is need to reflect anew on the concept of creation, because the term "from nothing" doesn't mean anything. We need to find new words to say what creation is. We know all about evolution, but almost nothing about creation. Christians themselves have problems with creation. Even at Louvain I did not talk so much about creation from nothing – a philosophical concept – as about participation.

I returned to this topic at the end of my university career. For two years I gave courses on creation. I analysed it in Genesis, I studied it in the Assyrians and Babylonians and in many other accounts. I found the same imagery as in Genesis. I traced a panorama of creation in patristics, in the Middle Ages, above all in St Thomas. I studied the war between evolutionists and creationists, attacking the concept of causality in relation to creation, which can be understood by someone who knows philosophy. But that is not a requirement for a Christian.

I have examined the concept of contingency and nothingness (*le néant*) in Sartre which led him not to accept God. Sartre makes a profound analysis of the contingent without accepting God. I asked myself: what is the difference between a believer's experience of contingency and a non-believer's experience of contingency? Is it the same experience?

A believer's experience of contingency is different from an atheist's experience of contingency because, simply keeping to the same experince of contingency, in fact this is an empty contingency. The experience of contingency without God is totally different from contingency related to God. This is a very delicate question. I have reflected a good deal in an attempt to find the right word, because the humanists have made me see that it is the same experience, so why then introduce the interpretation, which is a superstructure? But it is not in fact a superstructure because an atheist's experience of contingency is in fact an interpretative atheistic experience as such. It is an atheistic experience quite different from the experience of a believer. On the one hand it is the same experience of contingency, but on the other it is an experience which can be had differently by an atheist and a believer. I can see that it is very difficult to formulate thought.

At the end of my course I said that there is a difference between God and the creature, but the difference, the frontier, is not in God but in us.

The nucleus of my reflection on creation is the concept of experience, which at one time was not in fact accepted by atheistic philosophy. However, now, with Sartre, atheistic philosophy affirms the experience of human contingency. The creation is the experience of contingency, but in relation to God.

There is also a growing interest in creation in the theological field. Attention is drawn to the need to have experience of the created, of contingency. It is a profound need. One need only think of the New Age. I personally am against this type of interiorization of all problems. On the other hand, in all the currents of Christian mysticism there is in fact interiorization, though I think that it is not based on an anthropological perspective, because to get into oneself one has to go through exteriority. This is Thomism. Interiorization which blocks exteriority is for me a false course. It's empty. Interiorization and externalization cannot be separated. The dichotomy is a modern phenomenon which comes from Cartesian philosophy. Interiorization always happens through experience. Interiority comes to be filled from exteriority.

The dualism between spirit and matter changes the relationship with contingency and consequently with creation. So I am against all these currents: New Age, transcendentalism... It is difficult to find a place for Jesus Christ in them. There is in fact no need for Jesus Christ. There is no mediation of history here, only the void in this interiorization without externalization. To have no recourse to historical experience is to fall into the void, and without history our humanity is empty.

What is the psyche without externality? What is the anima without corporeality? For me creation is increasingly a Christian anthropology. When nature and the cosmos are taken up by human history, there is a balanced notion of creation. Otherwise, without the world, there is only a fictitious, imaginary, fantastic notion. Modern subjectivity cannot arrive at God by leaving nature aside. It has only a subjectivity and is perhaps imaginary.

The New Age is the apogee of modernity in its worst dimension. It finds only human spirituality important and interesting.'

'What is the relationship between prayer and interiorization?'

'Exercises of interiorization are not prayer. For a Christian and for the followers of the monotheistic religions, prayer is putting oneself before a person with whom one can talk and dialogue and to whom one can listen. In all these non-Christian mysticisms there is no relationship with a person but with a vague mystery. For us Christians it is God who reveals himself. In the New Age, in transcendental meditation, it is the individual who achieves the success; this is not the gift of grace. It is human beings who redeem themselves by descending to the depths of their being. But what do they find there? The void, perhaps. When that is done without nature and history, that's what happens.

In these movements there is undoubtedly a serious personal quest, but the solution is misleading. Be this as it may, there is a need to find why these phenomena arise and develop. Our spirituality, which has gaps in it, is certainly called in question. The true mystical currents are being forgotten. The church itself has often been mistrustful. In all the monotheistic religions, which are prophetic, mysticism is regarded with suspicion. There is a mystical current in Judaism; there is a mystical tradition in

49

Christianity, not to mention Islam. The monotheistic religions are mystical religions. The foundation of mysticism is the relationship with God as person. In the Eastern religions God is impersonal. For us, God is visible in human history in Jesus Christ.

For me, mysticism is the most intense form of the experience of God, which is on an equal footing with faith. It is essentially the divine life. It is not a reserved sector of the Christian life to which only some privileged people have access.

True mysticism is not a flight from the world, but, starting from an originally destructive experience, is an integrating and conciliatory sympathy with all things: an ardent approach, not a flight.

So the notion of creation is basic for understanding the history of salvation. Christ is concentrated, condensed creation. The whole Christ phenomenon is related to all creation. In Christ the creature is crystallized in a perfect way. It is the consequence of accepting the incarnation. God has become man. The man Jesus is the personal manifestation of God, but in the integrity of his humanity.

The creature Jesus is a concentrated, condensed creation whose whole participation with God is realized in a unique way, not realized in other human beings.

One can conceive of human beings without a relationship to God. This is what atheists do. But you cannot conceive of Jesus of Nazareth as a man without a relationship to God. That is the explanation of the three persons of the Trinity.'

THE TRINITY

'We approach this mystery groping and stammering. First of all, it relates to God who manifests himself in creation and, in a unique way, in the Jewish people as the people of God. Secondly, God manifests himself in Jesus, and then we talk of the Son of God. And thirdly, there is a manifestation of God in the life of the church and in all creation: this is the Holy Spirit. It is the same God, God in the Old Testament, God in Jesus Christ, God in the Holy Spirit, but they are forms of existence of God in history.

Christianity speaks of the divine Trinity. But I personally am somewhat reticent about the Trinity. I am afraid that saying that God is three persons risks producing a kind of tritheism: three Gods, three persons, like a kind of family. I hesitate to do speculative theology on the three persons and the relations between them. Through Jesus Christ, Son of God, there is the relationship with God the Father; after his resurrection, Christ is from God in the form of the Spirit, as an eschatological gift of God and God's. One can talk of the Trinity, but what does it mean to say three persons? I accept the personality of God, but we do not know the divine mode of this personality. The Trinity is God's mode of being personal. In this I am fully orthodox and in harmony with dogma.

That is what dogma calls for, because the three persons *qua* persons do not constitute the dogma of the Trinity as such. The Council of Toledo[1] speaks of *tres res* (three entities) in God: God is Trinity as regards the personality, the divine mode of being a person.

I am not a follower of "modalism", the theological doctrine of the second and third centuries, according to which the three persons of the Trinity are three forms of appearance of a single divine person: three forms of external appearance, towards the world, of one and the same person.

I reject "modalism", because for me the divine nature is trinitarian; it is personally trinitarian. I do not explicitly say three persons because that is ambiguous (tritheism), but I do say that the nature of God is itself personal with a trinitarian structure.

Divine personalism is a trinitarian structure. To speak of three persons can jeopardize the Trinity as such.

---

[1] The Eleventh Council of Toledo (675), which was not ratified by Pope Innocent III, as is often wrongly said, approved Augustinian formulations of the Trinity. What was involved was not a definition of the three persons as persons but the relationship between the Father, Son and Holy Spirit: 'three and one'.

There was no concern here to consecrate the term 'person' as such (it is the presupposition, and known to readers); the reaction was against tritheism ('There are not three Gods'), though the definition (which moreover is from a local synod) does not consider the term 'person' as such. The intention relates to the Father, the Son and the Holy Spirit, all of the same substance, and their reciprocal relations.

This is the first time that I have reflected on the Trinity in such an open way. For me the Trinity is God's mode of being person. I accept all the demands of dogma without running the risk of speaking of three persons, of a kind of family and in fact a tritheism which is popular in Christian faith.'

'Do you have any criticism of the theologies which now flourish around the Trinity?'

'To be truthful, I don't understand the speculation about the Trinity. I respect, for example, the speculations of St Thomas, but they do not speak in any way to my spirituality. There is too much speculation on the Trinity. Where is the saving value of all these speculations? Fr De Petter, my teacher in philosophy and my spiritual director, asked: "What sort of a thing is the Trinity? For me it is the trust that God manifests himself by saying that he is in three persons, but we don't understand it at all." This is to trust a mystery without saying that it is a mystery. God is Trinity (that is dogma!), but God is not three persons. That would be tritheism. I have never written on this subject because I'm afraid of it. I don't want to speculate, but I feel that there is something great here, something fascinating. There is a Trinity in the personal nature of God.'

'And what would be your confession of faith?'

'In the sense I have just described. I fully accept the creed, but the three divine persons are not in the profession of faith. I believe in almighty God, in Jesus the Christ, the beloved of the Father, Son of God *par excellence*; I believe in the Holy Spirit, who is the greatest problem for me. In the Bible the Spirit is a gift, not the third person; it is the very mode of being God, who gives himself to human beings. It is always the personality of God, but the personality of God in the history of the church, in the history of salvation.

The Father, the Son, the Spirit are the Trinity, a Trinity which cannot be split up as in the great treatises of St Augustine, St Bonaventure, St Thomas and, nearer to us, of Rahner and

Schoonenberg. In the end these are treatises which commit the sin of immodesty towards the mystery of the Trinity.

As for the Holy Spirit, I continue to be struck by the fact that when modern theologians tackle the question they say that theology has forgotten the person of the Holy Spirit. But at the end of their books I'm not much wiser about the Spirit. I know almost nothing. It is only true that he is like the wind, which blows where it wills and we don't know where it comes from. But the Spirit has effects. In essence the Holy Spirit is anonymous, and for that reason I find it very difficult to personalize. So I am very modest, almost agnostic, about a trinitarian theology. I confess the Trinity, but I have to be reticent about rationalizing the relations between the three persons.

Some of the great names of theology have also tackled the subject of the Holy Spirit, for example the great Fr Congar. Their treatises are certainly very interesting, and tell me a lot about God, but always about God. For me, when they talk about the Spirit, it is always the same God presented from different aspects and angles. The Holy Spirit is the bond between the Father and the Son: what does that mean? There is certainly a relationship between God and Jesus of Nazareth. It is an interpersonal relationship. But is this relationship between God and Jesus a third person? I ask myself. I am not against these speculations, but I do not find that they add anything to my spiritual life. I would say that they add nothing.

The personality of God, which is a personality with a trinitarian structure, a mystery that I accept, does not mean three persons as such. I repeat: it is not a dogma that we have to accept three persons. We need to accept the Trinity, but how does one accept the Trinity? There is the phrase *fides quaerens intellectum*, faith in search of understanding, but the intellect, the understanding, sets down a frontier and a limit for reason. The Trinity of many theological speculations is a rational Trinity and not a Trinity of the *fides quaerens intellectum*. It is a Trinity of reason. That's too much.'

'Do you prefer to stay with the mystery?'

'I confess the Trinity, but these speculations on relations between the three persons say nothing to me. The mystery cannot be rationalized, and when people like St Augustine, St Bonaventura, St Thomas, Rahner, etc., do rationalize it, the result is that these trinitarian theologies do not say anything about the mystery of God that is of any use to spirituality. They are pure rationalization; perhaps very interesting, but cold...'

HUMANKIND-CHRIST-GOD

'Human beings are in the image of God the Trinity. That is a fundamental affirmation. "Image of God" means that as in antiquity images of the Roman emperor were erected in all the countries of the empire to say "Here the emperor is the Lord", so God has done in creation. He has put the image of himself here to say, "I am the Lord, the sovereign of all creation." And human beings are the image of this God. Talk of God's representative means human beings as such. We are God's representatives throughout creation.

One can speculate about the image of God, but I think that, going back to the image of the emperor, the concept is very clear: "I am the Lord."

That human beings are the image of God means that humanity as such is God's representative. Human beings are God's image where and when they do justice, respect the integrity of creation, practise solidarity. It can be said that where God reigns, human beings have the right to be human. In their humanity men and women manifest the reign of God in history. And it is men and women who mediate the presence of the kingdom of God. Clearly the kingdom of God is God, the grace of God, the gratuitousness of God mediated through human beings. It is through this that anthropology and soteriology are connected.

Human beings are the image of God, and Christ is the pure image of God, as the Letter to the Colossians says. But there is a difference. In Jesus Christ the image of God is concentrated; in other words, Christ is the image of God with an exclusive uniqueness. Human beings can be considered autonomous in relationship to God, as atheists in fact are. Human beings are intelligible even without reference to God. The human fields are autonomous, and there can be an anthropology without God. But this is impossible for Christ as such. His humanity as such is related to God. It is the filial relationship with God that constitutes the humanity of Jesus. The humanity of human beings can be related to God in his autonomy. In Jesus Christ, too, there is human autonomy, but this autonomy is constituted by his filial relationship to God. Both Jesus Christ and human beings, though in different ways, are the image of God.'

THE GRATUITOUSNESS OF GOD

'In the third volume of your christology you talk of the gratuitousness of God in almost lyrical tones, which are deeply moving.'

'The essence of God is absolute freedom. In scholastic philosophy there is a distinction between the nature of God and the freedom of God. This is a distinction also made by St Thomas. The nature of God is not necessity but absolute freedom. It is in relationship to us that the nature of God is every moment new, because it is absolute freedom. It is a surprise at every moment of our life, even in eternity. It is an absolute surprise. So there is no distinction between the nature of God and his freedom. Otherwise the freedom of God is made free will, i.e. the capacity to choose between good and evil. And that would be a finite and limited freedom. However, the nature of God is infinite and absolute freedom.

That is why God is by nature purely gratuitous. And it is why it is impossible to prove the existence of God with rational arguments as such. All that we can say is that in our human life, both individual and communal, there are points, places, in which talk of God becomes intelligible. But the existence of God for us is purely gratuitous. And gratuitousness cannot be proved. It's enough.

At any moment it is new for us because it is gratuitous, it is absolute freedom. There can be places where talk about God is intelligible, but that does not prove the existence of God; it simply proves that there is a rational foundation to talk of God. Only the intelligibility of talk of God can be proved.

St Thomas with his famous five ways only wanted to explain that belief in the existence of God has a rational foundation and is therefore intelligible to human beings. So one can talk of God, and talk about God is not absurd: however, this is not proof of the existence of God.

I always talk of the gratuitous and absolute presence of God in relation to all creatures. Even if God remains silent, he is present, and we believe in the gratuitousness of this presence. Our experience can contradict his presence.'

THE HIDDEN AND SILENT GOD

'God's presence is fundamental, above all in reference to the presence of evil and suffering in the world. It is not that God wills suffering, but he remains present silently. In the moment of Jesus' death God was present, but silently. Death when God is silent is the supreme suffering. Those who believe in God know that God's silence is not absence. So one can trust in God even at a time of supreme silence.

This is the connection between anthropology and grace: the absolute presence of God is free and saving for human beings. God is not only a presence but a gratuitous, personal presence, so that you can talk to God, cry out your pain to him.

The absolute silence of God reveals his absolute presence.'

ATHEISM

'The absolute presence of God is a silent presence. One can remain in the experience of contingency, like the atheists, without going beyond it, without putting oneself in a relationship with God. When we say as Christians that God can remain silent, the possibility of atheism is a fact. The existence of this silent presence cannot be proved. Atheism is possible. In the Middle Ages and antiquity it was pure atheism, but in the modern period atheism rests on theoretical presuppositions. The silence of God can be interpreted as the non-existence of God. Atheism is a human possibility. There is a kind of rationality in atheism. The experience of human contingency can lead to God or can lead to denying him, not in fact sensing him. Neither theism nor atheism can be proved. They are part of the interpretative experience of reality. I refuse to say that atheists do not believe and that only the members of a religion are believers. All are believers, but their belief has different content. Through the experience of contingency, one picks up the gratuitousness of God and the other experiences nothing, the void. The experience of contingency confronts human beings with a choice: either belief in the gratuitousness of God or the rejection of a God who keeps silent.

Since the presence of God is absolute, it cannot be localized in our world. God embraces all creation. God is immanent and transcendent. God is word and silence.

Silence gives birth to prayer, but it can also make one aware of the void. The silent presence can be accepted, but without penetrating the mystery in a personal way. It is possible to have recourse to prayer understood as immersion in the mystery without asking anything, without engaging in dialogue with anyone. It is not the prayer of believers, but sheer immersion in the ocean of the infinite, a kind of mystic passivity. So in the face of the gratuitousness of God there are three possibilities: acceptance which leads to personal prayer, atheism, passivity. But we shall be returning to this in the next section.'

JESUS A FREE GIFT

'*You have said and written many times that Jesus Christ is the centre of your theological reflection. Some people are clearly perplexed by "your" Jesus. But who is he for you?*'

'Jesus is the free gift of God. The creation as such is a free gift of God, who has made human beings autonomous. The creation is the presupposition for entering into relations with God. God, in creating, has created human beings in their humanity, and

57

human beings in their autonomous spirituality can enter into a personal relationship with God. This relationship is called grace. There is a great difference between creation and grace. Creation is certainly a kind of grace, but it is not the grace of theologal life, which is the intense dialogue between human beings and God. Creation is setting the human being as an *other* over against God, and the two can enter into a reciprocal, intersubjective relationship. Intersubjectivity between the human creature and God is the life of grace. This presupposes the creation of human beings as persons who can enter into relationship with God. Before having an intersubjectivity and an interpersonality, i.e. the life of grace between God and human beings, it is necessary to be a creature. So there is a distinction between grace and creation. The covenant between God and human beings is intersubjectivity, the theologal life of human beings.

This theologal life is concentrated in a unique way in Christ, because in him there is a fullness of relations between Father and Son. Our theologal life is a participation in the life of Christ, in his filial relationship with God. We participate in the relationship between Father and Son; we are this relationship. Only Jesus is interpersonal relationship; we merely take part. Here is the uniqueness of Jesus Christ.

The Eastern religions speak of the relationship with God, but not of God's revelation. They do not know this concept. There is in them this mysticism of the human being who finds God within himself or herself; this kind of redemption brought about by human beings themselves, who enter into themselves and find God in their depths. It is human beings themselves who are the source of the relationship with God.

That is the great difference between these religions and the monotheistic religions in which God communicates as person. In the Eastern religions one enters into the mystery, which is often a kind of void. There is no prayer; one does not pray to God: it is simply a matter of putting oneself in the mystery. There is something fascinating in this, but only in the monotheistic religions is there a personal God to whom one turns in trust, like children who speak to their father.

On the other hand, even in Jesus' religious relationship, the experience is theocentric. God is the God of all human beings, wants the salvation of all men and women, and there are intermediaries for getting to God outside Christ. In the other religions one has access directly to God. If, on the one hand, the exclusivism that salvation is concentrated only in Jesus is unacceptable, on the other hand I affirm the absolute uniqueness of Christ in the history of religions, arguing for the positive value of the non-Christian religions, provided that they are humane. The criterion is their humanity. A religion which damages and destroys human beings and human dignity is a religion which denies itself. A religion which humiliates human beings is, by definition, a mistaken way of believing in God and at the least a religion which has lost any sense of its own interpretation and contact with its authentic roots.

These are very evocative ideas, which can be developed and deepened. Human suffering, the death of innocents, sickness, all these put in question the silence of God, who is present purely in a gratuitous way.

God who gives himself gratuitously, God who speaks by being silent and disquieting, I find all this fundamental to Christian spirituality. It can be said that the prophetic Christian religion is a religion of mystical abandonment and at the same time a religion of high prophecy which is committed to fighting against injustice for human liberation and happiness. Abandonment and commitment are the two pillars of the Christian religion, while the other religions are characterized more by abandonment. The commitment against injustice is essential for us. It is where Christ himself met his match. Even on the cross the Christian sees the gratuitous, eloquent, benevolent presence of God. God does not want suffering, which is in the very structure of creation. God is for conquering evil and injustice. Human beings can will evil, but God is not checkmated by this human will. God opposes it through the mediation of human beings, who are called to struggle against evil.'

HOLINESS AND PRAYER

'What is holiness for you?'

'It is the will of God communicated to human beings. We have to seek what is good. We have to experience good. Holiness is the awareness of the absolute and gratuitous presence of God; it is the commitment to others in justice and in love. It is human integrity, but taken up into intersubjectivity with God. I am not saying that to be Christian and to be human are the same thing, because one can be human without a living relationship with God, but holiness is a humane humanity taken up into the theologal life of God. Holiness and theologal life or the life of grace are the same thing. Faith, hope and charity are the virtues which relate directly to God. The theologal life presupposes and assumes ethical life, but the theologality is more than ethics and the Christian life cannot be reduced to the ethical life, which is clearly essential for Christian life.'

'And what about prayer?'

'Prayer has a mystical aspect; in other words it is the experience of the gratuitous presence of God; it is recognizing the presence of God. That is already prayer. But prayer also has a petitionary aspect, as we can see from the "Our Father".

We ask God for the coming of the kingdom; we ask him to do his will; we ask forgiveness for sins and ask for our daily bread. These are requests. Prayer in the monotheistic religions has the character of a request. We are asking for something for ourselves when we ask for the coming of the kingdom, which is human happiness, but in abandonment to the absolute presence of God. These two aspects are always present in prayer: praise of God, with the acceptance of his absolute presence, and the request for something for ourselves and for others.'

'*You have concentrated your reflections above all on human beings, on our relationships with one another, with God, with creation. Why so much interest in human beings?*'

'Human beings are the image of God. Where human beings are, there history is being acted out and constructed in a human way. God is working out salvation. Human beings are free beings, can write a history of sin but also a history of salvation. In constructing a history which exalts humanity, in this human commitment, it is God who gives salvation through human mediation. It is God who makes a history the history of salvation with human mediation.'

MARY: THE BIG SISTER OF CHRISTIANS

'*I hope it won't seem strange if at this point I ask you about the Virgin Mary.*'

'From immediately after the Council, over the last thirty years, there has been a kind of moratorium in mariology, and there has not been much talk about Mary. Now research is being resumed from other perspectives, putting the emphasis on the relationship between Mary and the Holy Spirit. This is the Mary of the Gospel, of the infancy narratives. There we find the foundations of mariology, not to forget St John, where we find the relationship between Mary and the Holy Spirit. We now have a christopneumatological mariology, which can also be accepted by the other churches because in their mariology this is the relationship between Mary and the Holy Spirit. All the mariological titles are ecclesiological titles. The litanies refer to the church. It seems to me that the ecclesiological titles also derive from pneumatological titles. The mother of the church is not the Holy Virgin but the Holy Spirit. Mary stands alongside the faithful, and since the Holy Spirit is the mother of all the members of the church, Mary is the big sister of all Christians. This is a feminist point of view; the emphasis is put on the 'sisterhood' of Mary rather on her motherhood of the church. The Council did not want to consecrate the invocation 'mother of the church'; it said only that some call

Mary 'mother of the church'. I think that we need to work out a pneumatological mariology.'

6

Eschatology

'Human beings are historical, put in history to make history. So their itinerary is an itinerary made with God because they are God's creatures. But it can also be an itinerary without God and even against God. Human beings are historical beings in relationship with the eternal God. This relationship between historical human beings and the eternal God also raises the problem of eschatology. Since life is a contingent life with a beginning and an end, can human beings survive? Can we see more here? Is there a life after death? Is there a heaven for human beings who have done good? Is there a hell for those who have done evil? The problem is raised by human historicity. Eschatology is the Christian response to all these questions. Eternal life is not something inherent in the nature of the contingent being. Even if human beings have a spiritual soul, it cannot be said that the spirituality of the human soul is the foundation of a life beyond life. This is not in fact a Christian idea but a Greek one. The foundation of belief in the resurrection, in eternal life, is the intersubjectivity between the eternal God and contingent human beings. So the foundation of human eternal life is theologal life, the life of communion with God, and not human spirituality.

That is why the New Testament always speaks of resurrection and not of the immortality of the soul. It is a Greek and pagan conception that spirituality as such must be the foundation of eternal life. Human beings are incarnate spirits who begin a way and then finish it. In the Bible it is not said that the spirit lives and the body dies. The theologal life, the life of grace, is the foundation of the resurrection, and this theologal life is stronger than death.'

'Let's use the language of the man in the street. What is heaven? What is paradise? What is hell?'

'Heaven and hell are anthropological possibilities. I argue that there is an asymmetry between the notion of heaven and the notion of hell: they cannot be put on the same level. If the foundation of survival is this relationship lived with God, I ask myself what happens when this relationship with God is not lived in any way, i.e. when a person does evil with final intent.

We do not know whether there are people who do evil in a definitive way, rejecting the grace and forgiveness of God; but if there are people – this is a hypothesis – who have no theologal relationship with God, these do not have even the foundation of eternal life. Hell is the end for those who do evil in a definitive way, their physical death and also their absolute end. So from an eschatological point of view there is only heaven.

This is something quite different from the *apokatastasis* or general recapitulation of Origen[1] and others. I repeat, I do not know whether there are people so evil as to reject the grace and forgiveness of God. It is possible that all human beings are destined for heaven, but all events, if there were perhaps wicked men and women, and I mean definitively wicked, their physical death would end their existence. There is only heaven – and not alongside hell, where human beings undergo fire and pain for all eternity. It is against the nature of the God who is love for human beings to be punished for all eternity. For me, a man of faith, it is unthinkable that while joy pervades heaven there should be people not far away on the point of expiring in the midst of infernal and eternal suffering. There cannot be a hell which is the opposite of the eternal joy of the kingdom of God. There is only the kingdom of God.

---

[1] A church author, who was born around 185 in Egypt, perhaps at Alexandria, and who died in Tyre around 253-4.

In the Christian world the *apokatastasis* was affirmed above all by Eastern fathers and by Origen, understood as the return of all creation to a state of utter felicity.

Heaven and hell are anthropological possibilities because human beings are finite, their freedom is finite, and they can choose either good or evil in a definitive way. This is an anthropological fact. I don't know whether there are these people who choose evil. But even if there are, hell does not exist.[2] There is no infernal life. If there are those who in their lives are capable of separating themselves totally and definitively from communion with the God of life, they are destined for the annihilation of their own being.

Some theologians say to me, "So is no one is punished for the evil that they commit?" I reply, "Not if they have a sense of what it means to be with God for all eternity." For such human beings, there would not be the life of communion with God... The wicked would not have the happiness of God for all eternity... It is terrible. God does not have feelings of revenge. For me this coexistence of eternal heaven for the good and hell for the wicked, who receive eternal punishment, is impossible. The "eschaton"[3] or the

[2] To clarify these somewhat shorthand expresssions and to make them comprehensible in the context of this review, I would refer to R.Gibellini, *La teologia del XX secolo*, Brescia 1992, 367f.: 'For Schillebeeckx, there is no symmetry between "paradise" and "hell", so hell cannot be a counterpart to paradise, as is generally argued in scholastic theology. But Schillebeeckx also refuses to accept the revision made on this point by theologians who do not belong to the "infernalist" (to use a term coined by von Balthasar) school, like Teilhard de Chardin, Rahner and Balthasar himself, who see hell as a real possibility for final error, but insist on the need to "hope for all". Schillebeeckx puts forward another solution: the logic of the good which is expressed in the praxis of the kingdom relates, on the basis of the promise and grace, to the final consummation of eternal bliss; however, the logic of evil is not relevant in any way, and if there is anyone who in his or her life is capable of becoming totally and definitively separated from communion with the God of life, he or she is destined to the annihilation of their own being: "But there is no shadow kingdom of hell next to the eternally happy kingdom of God...The 'eschaton' or the ultimate is exclusively positive. There is no negative eschaton. Good, not evil, has the last word. That is the message and the distinctive human praxis of Jesus of Nazareth, whom Christians therefore confess as the Christ" (E.Schillebeeckx, *Church: The Human Story of God*, 138f.).'

[3] The Greek term 'proton' means 'first', 'the beginning', the opposite to 'eschaton', last and end. Protology considers the religous (extra-scientific) conception of the origins of the world and humanity (the creation stories).

final fulfilment is exclusively positive; there is no negative eschaton. Good and not evil will have the last word. This is the
message and this is the praxis of the life of Jesus of Nazareth.'

'And purgatory?'

'The notion of purgatory is a Catholic notion, which I find
essential for eschatology. Even if human beings have chosen the
good and are to have an eternal life in heaven, they are not saints
like Jesus Christ. They have imperfections, faults. Even if a person
dies in a state of grace, as we say, he or she still remains a sinner.
In the first encounter in heaven with God, the God of holiness,
the first act of God's love is a kind of catharsis, purification. God's
first act of charity is the purification of all our imperfections.

In an instant. So purgatory is not a place, any more than hell
and heaven are, but a state which cannot be described. God's first
act of love in heaven is an act of illumination. God projects his
light on human beings, illuminates them and purifies them. It is a
kind of rooting in God, and the first moment of the beatific vision.
So all men and women go through purgatory before entering into
the beatific vision of God.

Purgatory, then, is not the fire of purification from sins. St
Thomas himself asked how a soul separated from the body could
be purified by fire. This is not the fire of punishent but the fire of
purification. The fire is only an image.

There are theologians who argue that eternal life is the earthly
life of those who believe, who are in communion with God. For
these, physical death is the end of human beings and there is no
life after death. One enters the bosom of God without a personal
existence. For these theologians life finishes, and there is no
relationship between the life led on earth and life in the bosom of
God. But in that case life is a farce. They talk of immortality and
survival, but after death, one disappears into God without one's
own, personal existence.

This is a theory which is unfortunately finding a following. I
fight against it because I cannot conceive that my physical life will
finish in anonymity, albeit divine anonymity.

The French Dominican Jacques Pohier adopts these positions,
though he now accepts the resurrection of Christ. That seems to

me to be even more nonsensical: on the one hand to accept the resurrection of Christ and on the other not to accept the resurrection of other human beings.

'But how do these theologians explain the words of the creed that refer to the resurrection of the flesh?'

'They say that in human beings there is an infantile desire for survival, as it were a form of megalomania. I too say that we do not have the right to have an eternal life, which is a free gift of God. St Paul says that without the resurrection life is empty. That is very true.'

ESCHATOLOGY AND PROTOLOGY

'Let me say something more about paradise. The Old Testament talks of eschatology with an eye to protology. Throughout Genesis, the idea of paradise and of the human beings who live there is a reflection of eschatology in protology. The creation is a projection of how the prophets conceived the idea of the paradise in which human beings had been placed. It is a transposition of the prophetic eschatology to the beginning of humanity. An effort was made to give an explanation of history in which God had spoken to human beings of salvation. The message of the prophets was transferred to the beginning of creation. God placed human beings in paradise, but they sinned, were driven out and began a story of sin.

The notion of paradise belongs to eschatology. The whole Genesis story is inserted into eschatology. For the Greek Fathers, human beings immediately start writing their history of sin. By contrast, the Latin Fathers described human beings in paradise, perfect beings who then sinned. This is a mystification in the Latin Fathers. In the thought of the Greek Fathers paradise is the future of human beings. Human beings go towards paradise. The whole of protology is set in an eschatological frame because it has been constructed with a view to eschatology. The prophets say that in the kingdom of God the lion and the young child will play together. St Augustine and the Latin Fathers refer these images to paradise. It is true that it was the intention of God that history should be like this, but it should be said that human beings did not begin endowed with knowledge and wisdom but that, beginning from sin, they are making their way towards the kingdom of God. So protology should be read in the light of eschatology.'

'And what is original sin?'

'The new theories on original sin have been condemned by Rome. Now it is better to keep quiet. I believe in original sin; I believe that there is a sin of the world, that the structures of the world are made by sinful human beings and that one comes into the world with sin. But sin is there before human beings. Human beings come into a world where there is sin. On the one hand they take their place in a history of salvation, but on the other they take their place in a history of sin. It is a sin which transcends the personal will of human beings. Our very situation is affected by human sin. The whole of our history takes place "from sin to sin", as the Council of Trent said. This is human history.

Human beings sinned in Adam, but in the Genesis stories Adam is not a historical person: he is all humanity. Sin came before our will. That is what was defined by the Council of Trent. The imagery obscures the notion of original sin. The Congregation for the Doctrine of the Faith is very open towards theories of original sin. It is the only dogma for which it accepts demythologization.

I believe in original sin, while other theologians argue that it is pure myth. For me the sin of the world, as St John calls it, is a reality. At any rate one must have the courage to demythologize protology to recover the nucleus of the story, which is that the sin of the world is a very powerful reality that overcomes our will and twists it towards evil.'

7

Ethics

'There is no such thing as a Christian ethic. St Paul says that we need to live "in the Lord". All St Paul's ethics are based on Stoic[1] ethics, above all when he refers to marriage. But St Paul adds that we need to live "in the Lord". It is an autonomous ethic, not a Christian, human ethic, but this autonomous human ethic must be lived in the light of the theologal life. Everyone, whether Christian or non-Christian, atheist or humanist, seeks norms. When everyone is looking for a solution, for example over abortion or euthanasia, the arguments are examined and in the end a "consensus" is achieved which is taken over into theologal life.

In history it has not always been the Christians who have understood where injustice is being done. Take slavery, for example. Christians accepted it. St Paul says, "As a Christian I am free, there is no distinction between slave and free, but in the life of society the slave must remain a slave." The letter to Philemon does not say that to be a slave in society is an evil. And this went on for centuries and centuries. It was not Christians as such who said that slavery was an evil. The human conscience said no to slavery. St Paul did not conclude that slavery is an evil. He could have deduced that from christology, but he didn't. Morality as such is autonomous, but it must be lived by Christians in a religous context. There is a kind of interrelationship between autonomous ethics and the Christian context in which autonomy is assumed.

For that reason I am against certain ethical positions in the

[1] One of the great philosophical schools of the Hellenistic period, so called from the 'portico' in which it was founded, around 300 BCE, by Zeno of Citium. It asserted the primacy of moral problems over theoretical problems.

official church which pass themseves off as Christian but which in fact are not, because they belong to a certain philosophy. One thinks in exasperation of the very rigid attitude to sexuality and marriage. The official church sometimes follows a particular philosophical current, scholasticism, which has a definite conception of human nature. Human and Christian ethical norms have human dignity as their foundation. That is the criterion in all fields of morality: Christians seek with others what is permitted or forbidden in the circumstances. With others we seek norms, not privileges.

There is no revelation in ethical matters; ethics is a human process. It is not God who says "This is ethically permitted or forbidden." It is human beings who with reflection and experience must say this and establish it. So there is no such thing as a Christian ethic.

Islam is another matter; that has its ethics.

For Christians neither revelation nor faith impose ethical norms, even if these are sometimes inspirations and orientations.'

RELIGION AND ETHICS

'Religion cannot be reduced to ethics. But there is a close link between faith and morality. Christianity perceives the autonomous ethic of humanity in the context of a practice in conformity to the kingdom of God, where its experience is set. The spirituality of Christian ethics, which as ethics is nothing more than moral autonomy with respect for human dignity as its scope, is set at the level of theologal life, i.e. is related to God. At all events ethics needs a God who is greater than ethics. The more we keep silent about this meta-ethical God, the first source and horizon of every ethic, and the more we declare him dead, the more we bind ourselves to false gods, to idols of our own making.

But God is not compatible with the idols; he is a jealous God who for the good of humankind never enters into conflict with his dignity. On the contrary, he raises it up and honours it.'

'What do you think of the attitude of the church to homosexuality?'

'There is no specifically Christian ethic about homosexuality either. It is a human problem, which must be resolved in a human way. There are no Christian norms as such for judging homosexuality. The American bishops have recently protested against Cardinal Ratzinger's letter on homosexuality. It goes against all the new insights of science. There are people who are homosexual by nature. What can we say to that? There is not yet a "consensus" on the matter, but to say that discrimination in social life is ethically permissible is not on; it is against Christianity. To appeal to the Bible to condemn homosexuality is unjust. I understand that there is need for much reflection and that we must proceed cautiously, but condemnation and discrimination are certainly not Christian. These people are suffering.

In conclusion, the notion of ethical autonomy, which must be lived "in the Lord", in a Christian context, has not yet been accepted by the church. What still counts is the conception of St Thomas, whose ethics are Aristotelian, based on pure rationality.'

8

The Ministries in the Church

'I am not against the institutions of the church. But they are human, historical institutions which had to evolve for the good of Christians. You can see that in the post-Pauline letters. The institutions are based on the fact that there is a church, but the institution as such is a human institution. For example, it cannot be said that bishops, priests and deacons were instituted by Christ. They are an evolution. It is from the second half of the second century that we have the episcopate, the priesthood and the diaconate as they are today. They are the fruit of a legitimate and positive evolution, but I do not see why they cannot change.

The documents of Vatican II – the Council of Trent had already referred to the question – do not say that the ministries are an institution of Christ. The Council of Trent said "by divine disposition", in other words they evolved historically by the action of God. Trent corrected the expression "by divine institution", preferring the expression "by divine disposition". Vatican II chose a third expression, *ab antiquo*, that is, from of old, because in fact the hierarchical articulation of the church took place in accordance with sociological laws. Beyond doubt there is a link to the historical Christ. The great exegete Descamps argued that the notion of the Twelve has a link with Christ. The church is the new Israel. In the community of the Twelve there is the Petrine ministry. It is a fact of the New Testament that the leader of the church is one of the Twelve. But how can the Petrine ministry be exercised? Can it, for example, be a triumvirate? Or a college? Or a synod? That is a historical question, subject to changes.

Vatican II talked of collegiality: Peter and the other Eleven rule the church collegially. As Botte has demonstrated, collegiality is a patristic notion. The *Nota esplicativa previa* of Vatican II sought to diminish the scope of collegiality: the Pope can also act without the college. At the time of absolute monarchies one could understand this, but now, in a time of democracy and pluralism, one cannot. Authority is necessary, but not authoritarianism. Power can be exercised in a democratic way, but not against the faithful. We need to listen to the grass roots.

Even if Christ did not directly institute the church because he believed that the end of the world was near and did not believe in a long history in time, in fact after his death the proclamation of the universal and definitive significance of the message and life-style of Jesus continued.

The image that the primitive church had of itself from the beginning was that of being the people of God at the end of time, when all the people of Israel would finally be united in the same faith in Jesus and in his gospel message. So Jesus simply handed down a movement, a living community of believers, aware of being the new people of God: the eschatological "gathering" by God first of all Israel and then of all humankind.

In other words, the church is a movement of eschatological liberation with the aim of bringing together all men and women in a single unity, in a single peace, peace among them, peace among the peoples, peace with the environment.

Ecclesiology therefore derives from this eschatological vision, from the eschatological message of Jesus.

The whole institution is a ministry for preserving the freedom of the children of God. The hierarchy is a service to the people of God. The episcopate has the task of seeing that the message of Christ maintains its integrity, but does not damage the humanity of Christians. There must be respect for the laws of the church, for canon law, but when it proves that these norms are not accepted by the faithful because they are regarded as inhuman, the laws must be changed. Conversely, if they are for the good of the faithful, they will be accepted.

The structure of the church is being demythologized, even if the institution is necessary to preserve freedom in the church. When the church offers itself for service, it is a church which is credible and is welcomed with sympathy.'

'The church today sins by omission. It has many opportunities in the world, which today looks to it. But Christians often do not feel understood by the hierarchy. The church is needed because without the church there would be chaos. To suffer from the church and through the church is part of our Christian life. But this does not mean that we should be silent. We must have the courage to criticize because the church always needs purification and reform.

I prefer an ecclesiology in a minor key, not a grand ecclesiology. Many Christians do not agree with the vision of a grand and powerful church. They are for a modest ecclesiology.

What is the centre of Vatican II? The church. That is neither God nor the message of God for all men and women. Perhaps we need a council which speaks of God in our own time. The Council meticulously considered the church, but left God in the background. The church should be more of an appendix, a corollary to what is said of God. When this happens, the church will have more of a voice in the world.

Gaudium et spes showed a concern for the world, even if now we see that it reflects that particular historical movement of great euphoria. Those were the 1960s.

In this sense Ratzinger is right when he says that *Gaudium et spes* is too optimistic. Those were the days of the *homo "faber"*, man the "maker", of a marvellous society. But Ratzinger is an Augustinian and his criticism reflects his conception of the world.'

'*How do you see the ministries in this church* semper reformanda?'

'In the church there are many ministries that have been received by the church. The triad of bishops, priests and deacons is being maintained by the church; but there are other ministries which can be received by an ordination, i.e. an official recognition on the part of the church. The separation of the triad from the other ministries is outdated because it is said that these three pertain to the clergy and the others to the laity. Even in the Netherlands people say: "The pastoral workers are doing marvellous, necessary work, but they are laity." But what does this mean? What does it mean to say that they are purely and simply laity? I ask myself this. In fact they do more than priests in the parishes. Often they are the ones with the community on their shoulders. Thus the priests are seen as the men of the sacraments. This is a dangerous reduction.'

THE NEW MINISTRIES

'It can be asked whether the seminaries are still worthwhile today. We know that they were institutions formed after the Council of Trent. In the Netherlands they were abolished after Vatican II, but now attempts are being made to reactivate them. While candidates receive a theological formation in the university, they do not also receive an appropriate spirituality. Sometimes this happens, but it is not the task of the theological faculties to give a spiritual and pastoral formation. There is need for a formation specific to the priesthood. How can that be done? In small communities, which are now being experimented with in many places. The major seminaries, the convents, the monasteries, are no use now; we need small communities with an adequate rule. The candidates are looking for a place of spirituality rather than a preconstituted seminary, with already predetermined rules. The candidates prefer to give themselves rules of life, rules which can change depending on the various needs. I can see that these communities have a future in the formation of the priestly ministry.'

VOLUNTARY CELIBACY

'In the course of our conversation, which has by now been a long one, you touched on the problem of celibacy. Do you want to add anything?'

'This is a question which, it seems to me, is increasingly a matter for the bishops, who continue to ask the Holy See to reflect seriously on the problem. There are cardinals and bishops who are asking explicitly for the law to be revised. On many sides there are requests that celibacy shoud be an option. In future, if celibacy is not made optional, there will be serious problems for the church. There are priests who have accepted obligatory celibacy and who continue to renew their choice, but there are so many others who no longer accept it and have relationships with women. That is understandable in an authoritarian church. It would be more honest to act openly. Both those who are married and those who are not are possible candidates for the priestly ministry. Celibacy is a charism. The priestly ministry is open to all Christians. I can understand people thinking, "If that happens, everything will collapse, there will be a catastrophe." But why? The Protestant church hasn't collapsed, nor has the Orthodox church or the Catholic church of the Eastern rite. Is their church less healthy? When will we see this? I do not know. It's such a waste of time. Many priests have left because of celibacy. Thousands and thousands. Why leave the people without the eucharist? Vatican II said that the Sunday eucharist is the heart, the soul, of Christian life. So why leave whole Christian communities without the Sunday eucharist?

That is a dramatic question which isn't receiving an answer.'

THE ORDINATION OF WOMEN

'In fact the women are more committed to the life of the church than the men. But they are deprived of authority, of jurisdiction. That is discrimination. Christ chose women, authentic apostles in their way. A woman was the first witness to the resurrection. The exclusion of women from the ministry is a purely cultural question, which doesn't make sense now. Why can't women preside at the eucharist? Because they can't receive ordination? There are no arguments against the ordination of women to the priesthood.

In a modern society women can fill any role, be in any post. And why isn't this allowed in the church? We need to prepare the people. When they're not prepared, grievous schisms are possible, which can be avoided. I personally am committed in my writings to informing people about these questions. And why not speak about it in homilies with much respect, kindness, serenity?

I followed on the radio the debate which took place at the General Synod of the Church of England on 11 November 1992. It was a debate at quite a high and profound level, with a marked pastoral concern for those in opposition, so as to maintain the unity of the church.

In this sense I am happy with the decision to confer the priesthood on women as well, and it seems to me that this is a great opening for ecumenism rather than an obstacle, because many other Catholics are going in this direction.'

THE RELIGIOUS LIFE IN THE LORD

'Let me say something about the religious life, which affects me closely since I am a Dominican brother. It is not a life separate from the Christian life. At all events it is the choice of a special way, which is pledged with vows.

The religious vows are possibilities of human existence in general. Even non-religious can live a celibate life because of a different choice, politics, for example. At the basis of religious life there are anthropological possibilities. The discussion here is the same as the one we had on ethics. There is an autonomous human possibility that one can live "in the Lord". Celibacy for the kingdom of God is a human possibility that can be lived in the Lord, with a view to the kingdom of God. Celibacy as such is not better than married life; it is just another human possibility, lived out by religious for the kingdom of God.

Thus only poverty as such is not a virtue. It is a human situation. One can live a life of poverty voluntarily to show solidarity with the poor of the world. So one can live in the Lord for the kingdom of God.

Obedience is purely a human possibility. One can live it in the Lord. So the religious life as a whole is a possibility, which can be lived communally for reasons which can be different from the kingdom of God.

These are possibilities of human existence which religious adopt for the kingdom of God. The religious life is the Christian life as such, but lived in a different way. It is a special state of life compared with the life of the Christian community, but it cannot be said that this life is something more, something which transcends Christian life. It is often said that the religious life is a superior life. I don't think so. It is an accentuation, a human possibility in the religious perspective. The religious pledges himself or herself to the world in a special way by putting the emphasis on the eschatological character of the Christian life, not escaping from the world. The religious life – orders, congregations, institutions – is an eschatological sign, and thus has a certain critical function towards the world and the church. In history the religious have always had this critical function, above all towards the church, as a result of which they are often *enfants terribles*, going against the current. They stimulate and criticize the church.'

'*How do you explain the current crisis in religious life?*'

'People say that it is because of a lack of the religious sense. I don't believe that. On the contrary, I can see the religious sense growing in the world. It can't be said that in the West we are the victims of secularization. It is rather that the institutional church has not understood how things are in some respects. Rather, I see this crisis of the religious life as a reaction to the supernaturalism of the religious life, understood as a flight from the world, as finding safety from the misfortunes of the world. Today there are many young Christians in the Third World and they are lay. There are new priests, new missionaries. Those who at one time became priests and missionaries now act as laity. It's only a shift, not a loss of the religious sense. It is always clear that the religious sense must be incarnated in humanity and thus in social solidarity if it is to change the structures. There are many lay Christians who are involving themselves in the world. At one time this role was filled only by priests and religious. So this is a shift, not a loss.

This crisis heralds new times. There is a need not so much for new orders, congregations, institutions, as for new orientations of these which will clearly bring a change to their very structures. For example, very few brothers live in this convent, the Albertinum, which is grand and huge. It's had its day. For me this is a crisis of growth, the *aggiornamento* of the religious life.'

9

The Confession of a Theologian

'In the introduction to the third volume of your christology, Church: The Human Story of God, *you write: "I hope that the book will be useful to many people. As far as I am concerned, it is a Christian confession of faith of a consistently rational theologian, who is conscious of standing in the great Catholic tradition on the basis of which he may be able to, indeed has to, say something – as an offer – to his fellow men and women." What do these remarks mean, now we are coming to the end of our conversation?'*

'I am one hundred per cent rational. I am against the faith of the enthusiasts. Some time ago Ratzinger said that we need to have a rather ingenuous faith, that we should not reflect much on faith... As if reflection on the faith was the task only of the hierarchy! As a believer I am rational, and look for rational arguments. In that way I feel myself one hundred per cent a believer. That is not a contradiction, as some people have remarked to me. To be a believer does not mean that one is irrational. Faith is the confession of a rational person. The rationality of faith must always be explored and clarified. All my theology is the theology of a believer: *fides quaerens intellectum*, faith in search of understanding. Human reason is used one hundred per cent in the field of faith. To bring in obedience and shut your eyes is neither Christian or Catholic. Believers need to be rational. St Thomas is a saint in his rationality because he used reason to confront faith. There is more and more need for rationality, above all to react against the fundamentalism[1] which is increasingly threatening the

---

[1] An American movement which began at the end of the nineteenth century. In the name of a radical and absolute fidelity to the Bible it opposed all interpretations based on scientific methods which favoured a purely verbal exegesis.

churches. The fundamentalism which is also present today in some Christian communities leads to obscurantism. It is a great danger, because human reason is denied.

Certainly human reason cannot be left to itself, because if it is, there is a danger that it will end up as sheer positivism. Faith develops a critical and corrective function so as not to lapse into rationalism and shut out the mystery. Without human reason faith becomes fundamentalism. Both faith and reason develop the function of mutual criticism.'

'How do you rate your theological activity?'

'It was once said of theological schools that there were masters and pupils. That is no longer the case. The idea of having a school has been superseded. The great syntheses which used to remain for several centuries are no longer there. I don't write for eternity, but for the men and women of today who are in a particular historical situation. I try to respond to their questions. So my theology has a date; it is contextual, but at the same time I want to go beyond the situation as such. That is a universal aim of my works because I try to take into account the questions of all men and women. Otherwise it wouldn't be good theology. The relevance of a theology is not an ephemeral relevance. Other theologians will see to other times.

I am content to have said something for the men and women of today, and perhaps also something that will interest the next generation. When a theology can nourish the next generation it is a great theology, which continues the great theological tradition.'

I AM TRULY A HAPPY MAN!

'It is difficult to trace a clear dividing line between my personal life and my life as a theologian. Both these aspects have developed within this cell in the Albertinum and in the University of Nijmegen, where I have now been for more than thirty years.

Two biblical texts have sustained me and still sustain me: the saying of St Peter, "Always be prepared to make a defence to anyone who calls you to account for the hope that is in you" (I Peter 3.15b), and the saying of St Paul, "Do not quench the Spirit, do not despise prophecies, but test everything; hold fast what is good" (I Thessalonians 5.19-21).

It is the Spirit which speaks through these two sacred texts. On the one hand, in my continual attempt to reorientate myself in the unexpected directions in which the Spirit of God breathes, this same Spirit has given my theological work a character of hope which is liberating and constructive, which, from what my readers have told me, verbally and in writing, to my great joy, opens up people's lives.

On the other hand the Spirit has been a pure source of the inexhaustible critical character of my writings, of the critical attitude which in the course of these thirty years down to the present day has led me to receive a certain number of letters in which Christian brothers have termed me a "devil in flesh and blood" and "a wolf in sheep's clothing", "a heretic of the worst kind" and "an immigrant to the Netherlands who for the good of the church and society would do better to go back to his own country".

My academic work still represents for me, in a very meaningful way, a form of apostolate and in particular a form of Dominican preaching of the Good News: the gospel of Jesus, the Messiah of the liberating God, chosen in advance by the Spirit.

However, in the meantime I have learned by experience that if religion is the greatest good of human beings and for human beings, it is often used completely to humiliate and even to torture people (in body and spirit).

So above all, in most recent years, in my theological thought I have preferred to defend human beings, men and women, against the dehumanizing demands of religion, rather than defend religion against the illusory demands of the sinful men and women that we are.

In these two aspects, the critical and constructive aspects of my theological thought, I have sought to bear testimony to others about the hope and joy within me. I am truly a happy man. I also much appreciate the freedom that my Dominican superiors, both Flemish and Dutch, have abundantly granted me from the beginning, to the great benefit of my theological work.'

Don't Be Afraid!
(The Prayer Psalm)

'I asked the Dutch poet Huub Oosterhuis to compose this prayer psalm for me, and I would like to use it to close these days of conversation in which I have dictated the testament of a theologian, passionate for God and for human beings.'

Are you a God at hand
and not a God far off?

Jer.23.23

Truly you are a hidden God.

Isa.45.15

Or do you hide your face from us,
to see what our end will be?

Deut.32.20

And yet
you do not willingly afflict
or grieve us.

Lam.3.33

You are ready to be sought
by those who do not ask for you;
you are ready to be found
by those who do not seek you.

Isa.65.1

Do I look for you in chaos?

Isa.45.19c

I hear you saying, Lord:
'I, the Lord, speak salvation;
and declare what is right.'

Isa.41.19d

But the poor and needy seek water
and there is none
and their tongues are parched with thirst.

Isa.41.16

How can my soul wait in silence
for you, God, who are my salvation?

Ps.62.1

May you find people, Lord, who work for justice.

Isa.64.5

Then we shall be able to say to everyone:
You are your God.
You set people free.
You have heard my cry.

You have heard me and said:
'Do not fear!'

Lam.3.37

'Behold, I am doing a new thing;
now it springs forth – do you not see it?'

Isa. 43.19

Lord, I believe;
help my unbelief!

Mark 9.24b

I am a poor fool, Lord,
teach me how to pray.

(Guido Gezelle)

The Principal Works of
Edward Schillebeeckx
(available in English)

(Dates of original Dutch publication are in brackets)

Revelation and Theology, Theological Soundings I (1964), Sheed and Ward 1967

God and Man, Theological Soundings II (1965), Sheed and Ward 1969

Christ the Sacrament [of the Encounter with God] (1959), Sheed and Ward 1963

Mary, Mother of the Redemption (1955), Sheed and Ward 1965

Marriage: Human Reality and Saving Mystery (1955), Sheed and Ward 1964

God the Future of Man, Sheed and Ward 1969

World and Church, Theological Soundings III (1970), Sheed and Ward 1971

The Mission of the Church, Theological Soundings 4 (1968), Sheed and Ward 1973

The Understanding of Faith, Theological Soundings 5 (1974), Sheed and Ward 1974

Jesus: An Experiment in Christology (1974), Collins and Crossroad Publishing Company 1979

Christ: The Christian Experience in the Modern World (1977), SCM Press 1980 (US title: *Christ: The Experience of Jesus as Lord*, Crossroad Publishing Company 1980)

Interim Report on the Books Jesus and Christ (1978), SCM Press and Crossroad Publishing Company 1980

Ministry: A Case for Change, SCM Press 1981 (US title: *Ministry: Leadership in the Community of Jesus Christ*, Crossroad Publishing Co 1981)

The Church with a Human Face: A New and Expanded Theology of Ministry, SCM Press and Crossroad Publishing Company 1985

Church: The Human Story of God (1989), SCM Press and Crossroad Publishing Company 1990

'Come and Visit me in Ghent'

Dear Edward,

I read with great pleasure your kind and honest letter of the 14th of this month and do not want to delay in perhaps doing you a service. First of all, please accept my warmest good wishes over the way in which the Lord has granted you the grace of the noble desire to dedicate yourself wholly to him and to the cure of souls. My prayers are with you and for you, that you may be able to continue along the way and understand clearly which order to choose so as to realize your ideal. I have the impression from your letter that you have already read something about the order of St Dominic: you know that it is an order of monastic priests and apostles whose orders are *contemplata aliis tradere* and whose motto is *veritas*. I would gladly give you a complete picture of the order and an exhaustive reply to all your questions, but that might be too hazardous. I personally feel so happy in the white habit of St Dominic that I do not want to embarass someone who might perhaps have the same vocation. So I prefer to acknowledge that in a few lines I can only list some boring facts. Perhaps you could come here some time to discover something about our order and, even more important, to share our life for a few days. You would learn far more from that than from all the books and all the letters, because there are things that you need to experience or to see at close quarters to get some idea of them. In that way you could easily discover whether your place is here with us. You could come, for example, from the Saturday afternoon of Pentecost and stay until the Monday.

Here is a brief reply to all your questions:

1. *Study among the Dominicans.* Our order is known as *the* order for study. That has been the case from the beginning. To promote study the superiors are obliged by the Dominican rule to give some dispensation to brothers, for example from fasting or from the night office. Study, like the life of prayer, is the main thing: the order is founded on prayer and study.

2. We study principally philosophy and theology, with other associated disciplines, like sociology.

3. Since the order is above all occupied with advanced studies, the Dominicans have founded few colleges. In France Fr Lacordaire has instituted a congregation of tertiaries of St Dominic to teach in the colleges. Recently the third order has been put on the same level as the first. In the Netherlands we have a large college at Nijmegen. Here in Belgium a college will probably be founded in a few years near Antwerp.

Many Dominicans teach in university institutions, as in Rome (the Angelicum), Freiburg, Nijmegen and so on.

4. As well as the Mass, as true monks we recite the hours, day and night.

5. The order has missions throughout the world. Our province has one in the Belgian Congo, 'In den Uele', founded in 1911.

6. Here in brief is the curriculum of a Dominican father:

(a) Postulant (after completing secondary school and an entrance examination): ten days.

(b) Vesting. Immediately after the beginning of the novitiate; the novitiate lasts one year.

(c) First profession of three years. Three years studying philosophy. Then the solemn, definitive profession.

(d) Four years of theology at Louvain. Ordination to the priesthood during these years of study.

(e) At the end of these studies the best students are sent to other universities to specialize in some subject (Rome, Freiburg, Jerusalem, Louvain).

7. The timetable here at Ghent is not very different from other houses.

At night, at three o'clock there is mattins and lauds (about an hour). At 6.15, there is prime and meditation till 7, when there is

mass. From 8.15 to 11.30 there are lessons. At 11.30, terce, sext and none. At 12.00 lunch with recreation until 1.30. Then follow vespers and lessons or study.
(Two passes a week, Monday and Wednesday.)
6.45 Supper and recreation until 7.45.
7.45 Compline and praise.

We have monasteries at Louvain, Ghent, Antwerp, Brussels, Ostend, Lier, Tienen and La Sarte. A house will soon open at Genk, near the coal mines. The Flemings remain in their area; we have two novitiates for Flemings, here in Ghent, and there is just one novitiate for French speakers at La Sarte (Hui). There are also two monasteries here for philosophy, the same ones. All the students subsequently go to Louvain for theology. There the language is optional and the lessons are given in Latin. There is some material in Flemish for the Flemings and in French for the Walloons. So the question of language does not present any difficulty for us.

There, dear Edward, are some facts. If you cannot come here and want more information, I will convey as much as I can. In any case I advise you not to take any decision before becoming much more informed about the Dominican life. But I have the impression from your letter that the white habit of St Dominic would suit you well. However, this is only an impression and should not influence your choice. Perhaps it might serve to convince you to pay a visit to the monastery of Ghent, where many brothers would welcome you in the love of Christ.

Receive, dear Edward, with my priestly blessing the assurance of my great desire to make you happy.

S.M.Matthijs
Prior of the Dominicans
Hoogstraat 39, Ghent

P.S. I have used a typewriter so as not to trouble you with my calligraphy.

In memory of
Marie Dominique (Marcel) Chenu OP
(7 January 1895 – 11 February 1990)

Marie-Dominique Chenu has died at Saint-Jacques in Paris: he was ninety-five. He had been practically blind for about ten years and had difficulties with breathing, but his spirit was keen to the end. The funeral took place in Notre Dame: the concelebrants were Cardinal Lustiger of Paris; Damian Byrne, the Master General of the Dominican order; Fr Marneffe, provincial of Paris; and six bishops. Several hundred Dominicans came from all over France and abroad to fill the two transepts, and the nave was packed with the faithful, who were deeply moved. During the celebration a telegram was read out from the Pope, through Cardinal Casaroli, in which the Pontiff expressed gratitude for all that Chenu had done for the church.

Well before the 'theology of hope', 'political theology', 'economic theology' and the various branches of liberation theology, Chenu had initiated theological renewal. Étienne Gilson once said, 'There is only one Fr Chenu each century'. One does not know which to admire more: his creative genius or his warm and human heart. Claude Geffré rightly wrote on the occasion of his death: 'Chenu was a master of theology and humanity' (*Témoignage Chrétien* 238, 19-25 February 1990).

In 1913, Chenu entered the monastery of Le Saulchoir (a house 'by the willows') of the French Dominicans in the neighbourhood of Kain in Belgium, because many monastic orders were then banned in France. He also studied for a period in Rome and returned to Kain in 1920. He cultivated his historical sense with Fr Mandonnet and Fr Lemonnyer, then dean of the faculty of Le

Saulchoir, where the great exegete Fr Lagrange was also teaching. In 1932 he was appointed '*regens studiorum*', master of studies, and successively rector of two faculties. Shortly before the war the monastery of Le Saulchoir was transferred to Etiolles, near Paris, and deployed in a new, fortress-like building. In 1942 the first blow fell on Chenu. The innocent and brilliant book *Le Saulchoir. Une École de Théologie* (1937) was condemned by Rome: the result of sinister moves, as Chenu well knew. From then on he never set foot in Le Saulchoir again.

Some years later, he was asked by the École des Hautes Études of the Sorbonne to give a weekly lecture on the Middle Ages. I myself went to his lectures in the academic year 1945-1946. His publications on the Middle Ages are all the fruit of these lectures. It was the great mediaeval master himself, Jacques Le Goff, who, in the name of the Sorbonne, the École des Annales and the Parisian mediaevalists, paid homage to Fr Chenu during the funeral liturgy. I would like to quote a sentence from Le Goff's oration: 'Fr Chenu taught me, as perhaps many historians would have liked to do without being capable of it, to clarify the development and activity of religious thought in history, putting these at the centre of universal history, where, without depending on it, they can find a place between economic history and social history, the history of ideas and church history in all their material and spiritual dimensions.' The non-believer Le Goff was the only one to applaud warmly in Notre Dame. All present heard it: the post-humous honour to the great master Chenu was more than deserved. Le Goff ended by saying: 'Farewell, Father. Thank you for what you have been, for what you have said, for what you have written, for what you have done. But you remain with us in spirit and in our hearts because we still need you.'

We must not forget that Chenu was anything but a student living outside the world. He was also the great inspiration behind the French worker priests. Because of this, in 1954 he was exiled from Paris on the intervention of the Vatican. This is a sorry story which has been evaluated and analysed in minute detail in the recent study by Fr Francois Leprieur, OP, *Quand Rome condamne. Dominicains et prêtres-ouvriers*, Paris 1989. Chenu did not practise a 'speculative theology'. He was a theologian on the basis of facts, events, movements of the past and the present. He was a researcher: always involved in research, like no one else, into the 'signs of the time' (see his article 'Les signes du temps' in *Nouvelle Revue Théologique* 97, 1965, 29-39). So his theology was very lively and present everywhere: at the birth of the Jeunes Ouvriers Chrétiens by Joseph Cardijn as early as 1933, when Chenu was living in Belgium; at the foundation of the reviews *Esprit*, *Sept* and *Témoignage chrétien*; at the institution of the Mission de Paris and the Mission de France; and finally at the foundation of *Concilium* in 1962. At a very advanced age he could still write a brief *magnum opus, La doctrine sociale de l'Église comme ideologie* (1979), in which he analysed all the social encyclicals of the Popes. Together with his brother in the order, Yves Congar, Chenu drafted the text of a 'Message of the Fathers of the Council to the World' in the years of Vatican II, speaking of the church of the poor. With many amendments, and very much watered down, this message was sent to the world. The message is then said to have inspired the first liberation theologians in Latin America, above all Gustavo Gutiérrez.

After his condemnation Chenu chose to go to live at Saint Jacques, becoming a pivot in the intellectual and spiritual life of the university city. Every Saturday afternoon, half the clergy of Paris would go to St Jacques, where Chenu would talk about the new books, giving authoritative advice on what books to read or not read. It was a kind of forum at which Chenu, like St Thomas in his *Quodlibeta*, responded to all the questions of the clergy of Paris. I often went to this event: it was truly an event, something like a mediaeval tournament, with a touch of vanity and ingenuousness.

I learned from Chenu that 'to think' is sacred: 'It is the intellectual which contains the spiritual.' Indeed, most of all, I am still surrounded by the great communicative warmth of Fr Chenu. He was a man of hope, an optimist of grace. So he was a Thomist through and through.

On Chenu's seventieth birthday there were celebrations in the presence of Cardinal Feltin. He praised Chenu for having accepted humbly and without disobedience the sanctions imposed by

Rome. Chenu jumped up and said: 'Eminence, it was not obedience, because obedience is a somewhat mediocre moral virtue. It was the faith that I had in the Word of God, compared with which clashes and passing incidents are nothing; it is because I had faith in Jesus Christ and his church.' That is Chenu: a man to love.

Mutual Love as a Commandment to live 'That Day' (John 14.20)

Fifth Sunday in the Year (year C)
Reading: Acts 21.1-5d; John 13.31-35
Albertinum, 17 May 1992
President of the Assembly:
Edward Schillebeeckx

To understand what is called the 'new commandment' of love we must call to mind the situation in which the Christian communities of the Johannine tradition found themselves after the disappearance of Jesus: Christ had been taken away and killed; what would happen next? In this Gospel the new commandment, a commandment to love to the death, is the reply to the problem of the physical absence of Jesus (John 13.33-34).

According to the Gospel of John the death of Jesus is on the one hand 'the victory of the prince of this world' (14.30, cf. 12.31) and on the other, according to its true and real significance, the return of Jesus to his 'Father's house', his return home (7.34-36; 8.21-22; 13.33-36). For the Johannine tradition the passion, death and resurrection of Jesus, his being seated at the right hand of God and the sending of the Spirit, the Spirit of Jesus who on that day – the precise moment of 'his hour' – with the Father, in the Spirit, on the day of Pentecost, comes definitively to 'dwell' among his disciples, constitues a unique and indispensable event. It is the glorification or sanctification of the name of God in Jesus, and by means of that at the same time the glorification of Jesus through God. According to the Fourth Gospel our brotherly love is present testimony, visible, effective, almost tangible participation in the unique liberating coming of Christ. The love of God is an event which God can bring about only in us and by means of us, if we achieve a love like that of Jesus; if necessary to the death – but preferably not.

The new thing which is spoken of in the Gospel of John, in the farewell discourse of Jesus who before his departure gives his disciples the commandment to love as a commandment of life, does not contrast with the precepts of the Old Testament covenant. Already at the basis of this commandment there is an element of newness: just as Jesus possibly needs to be ready to sacrifice his own life to remain faithful to that love if no other life can be led without betraying his own commandment of life. For that reason the last letters of John, which show a changed situation in the Christian communities, emphasize that such a commandment of love is concretized in the observance of God's commandments and in discipleship of Christ. Ultimately the two aspects of these letters are a reaction against some members of the community of believers who maintain the Johannine religious heritage in a unilateral mystical direction, and thus bring about a break between the original Johannine, authentically Christian, mystical enthusiasm 'of the reciprocal presence of God in human beings and human beings in God' and the painful and humiliating way of the cross that Jesus has to follow. (This break, quite apart from its 'dogmatic foundation', also has to do with an argument and a rivalry within the Christian community over the fact that Peter, traditionally the supporter of a very different line in the early church, was led to a martyr's death for the cause of Jesus the Christ, while the mystical 'apostle whom Jesus loved', who stands at the beginning of the community which lived according to the Johannine tradition, died in an ordinary way without any form of martyrdom. In a key passage which was later added to the Gospel of John [cf. John 21.18-23] there is a clear allusion to this rivalry.)

The meaning of the death of Jesus on the cross is diminished by a certain group within the community. These Christians combined the sanctifying gift of eternal life, which in fact throughout the Johannine tradition already begins on this earth, with the incarnation of Jesus as such, through his 'descent from above' and his being filled with spirit, his 'heavenly origin', and did not take into account his human response to the call to do the will of God, a life which in the end led to a humiliating death. However, this was a death which was transformed by the love of Jesus into liberating salvation for all of us (I John 4.7-11; John 3.16).

All in all, we can now say that some members of the community shared a certain frivolity of life with all those who keep on interpreting wrongly St Augustine's saying, 'Ama et fac quod vis: Love and do what you like.' The letters of John react against a false application of such a saying and, if they are understood rightly, sum up in themselves our whole commandment of life which is combined with both the promises and the commandments we have already received: in the 'word' of God or in what are called the 'Ten Commandments'. According to this Fourth Gospel, this is not only a betrayal of the spirit of the commandments itself, but also makes the biblical commandment to love quite different from what Jesus had intended and taught from the beginning of his preaching. I John says: 'Beloved, I am writing you no new commandment, but an old commandment which you had from the beginning; the old commandment is the word which you have heard' (I John 2.7-8). In other words, from the beginning the commandment to love given by Jesus, combined with the observance of God's commandments, is the heart of the Christian message: the mystical exaltation in God and the ethical commitment to defence of the neighbour which are typical of John belong closely together. The former cannot exist without the latter (even if by the term 'neighbour' this sectarian Johannine tradition meant only, or almost exclusively, Christian brothers).

Up to this point the true scope of the concept of the love as a new commandment of life as the Fourth Gospel understands it has not been fully disclosed. It is clear that while the Synoptic Gospels speak of the last supper and the 'new covenant' in the body and blood of Jesus, in its account of the last supper the Fourth Gospel never mentions the so-called institution of the eucharist as a memorial of the 'new covenant' but instead speaks of the service of washing feet, explaining this gesture as a symbol of the new commandment. The newness of this love has something to do with the new covenant of which the other Christian traditions speak.

The word 'new' – whether applied to the covenant or the command for mutual love – in both cases refers to the same truth.

It expresses something which is typical of Jesus and also of John. Given the human condition, God's covenant with men and women, with his people, is by definition always a new covenant. It is essential for God's eternal covenant with fragile and mortal human beings always to be a new covenant, even in the Old Testament, and always to remain new, in the sense of being a renewed covenant (Jer.31.31-34). 'Covenant' simply denotes Israel's obedient relationship to God's sovereign and free devotion to human beings, in a typical and characteristic situation of humanity, namely the situation in which Israel had broken off and kept on breaking off the free relationship instituted by God. There is no escaping the fact that just as the Gospel of John talks of the newness of the commandment to love, so repeatedly, and more than any other Gospel, it speaks of the 'sin of the world'. For Johannine thought the reference is not so much to the 'world' as the good creation of God as to 'this world', the theatre of the struggle between good and evil, between life and death, a world in which evil and death seem to triumph: 'the whole world is in the power of the evil one' (I John 5.19). Today more than ever, on the basis of scientific analysis, we know that every human being enters a world many aspects of which are already structured on a human, collective and social level. Apart from having a painful personal aspect, evil also has a historical structure; it is an anonymous power. Because of such a structure 'this world' is the source of discrimination and marginalization, a world of brute force, a sphere of life full of enmity and the exclusion of others. Translated into modern terms, the Johannine expression 'this world' means the world economy, the systems of government and the geo-political power relationships and all that they bring: injustice, poverty and pain, violence and death, and finally the destruction of nature. This is the sin of the world. Apart from the physical (or even physiological) connotations of the term 'original sin', we Christians cannot ignore (above all today, though some would prefer to) the sinful structure of our cultural and social heritage, a structure which precedes our personal work and our faults and which at the same time is inevitably the result of them. The dimension of original sin is simply a harsh aspect of our everyday reality which cannot be done away with simply by a sophisticated modern theology. It has been like this from the beginning of our history; it was like that at the time of the Johannine community. It is still like that, except that today with our means of communication we are confronted with the continuation of such a reality on a world level as well as on a local level.

According to the Gospel of John, Jesus too found himself on a similar battlefield, in a vulnerable position between the forces of good and the forces of evil. Jesus made a clear choice for justice and love, against the forces of evil. His way of living shows it. He attacked the temple that had become a place of trade and benefit to the Roman invaders and the priestly class of the Sadducees (John 2). He attacked the prejudices of the Judaeans who seized on God as though God was their property, excluding the Samaritans as heretics (John 4). He opposed the blindness of some Pharisees who put the law above human life (John 5 and 9). He opposed the violence of the moral system which was the cause of death as well as pardon (John 8). God, too, takes part in the struggle and is committed to it. God seems to stand on Jesus' side. According to Jesus, the Gospel of John's Son of man, whoever works for freedom, truth and life does the work of God. However, according to the eighth chapter of this Gospel, anyone who creates slavery, lies and death plays the devil's part (John 8.31-44). This Gospel of John, with its two faces, has not yet been filtered through the modern Enlightenment and does not know the modern shading. Everything is black or white, good or evil. There is no middle way. But despite all the legitimate criticism of the conceptual universe of this Gospel, despite its undeniable sectarian leanings bound up with a particular situation, exclusively within the church, reading it remains a dangerous and provocative memory for us. This Gospel account, which is decidedly esoteric for us, speaks of a God who makes a covenant with a humanity which keeps on sinning, while for his part he remains consistently faithful to his unconditional promises, despite the continual failings and weaknesses of human beings. God does not haggle with human beings. God does not say, 'If you do this, I, God, will do that.' God does not lay down conditions, but is generous without reason and remains faithful to such irrationality. So God sees human beings as continually sinners. God is faithful to his covenant, which is always surprisingly new. As Paul already wrote: 'He loved us while we were still sinners' (Rom. 5.8), and I John says: 'In this is love, not that we loved God, but that he loved us and sent his Son to be the expiation for our sins' (I John 4.10). Finally, a post-Pauline tradition in the letter to the Christians at Ephesus also says the same thing: 'But God, who is rich in mercy, out of the great love with which he loved us, even when we were dead through our trespasses, made us alive together with Christ' (Eph. 2.4). The eternal covenant of God with humankind is in fact new every day for sinful men and women.

Finally there is still a very delicate feature in the account in the Gospel of John that we have heard in today's liturgy. The Gospel expresses it in terms which are very mysterious to us, in the context of a mystical cultural setting on the fringe of Judaism with which few of us can identify.

During the last supper, shortly after Judas had gone out to betray Jesus, according to the contemplative reflection of the Fourth Gospel on all that happened to Jesus according to the tradition, Jesus said: 'Now is the Son of Man glorified, and in him God is glorified; if God is glorified in him, God will also glorify him in himself, and glorify him at once' (John 13.31-32). After these mysterious words, which are there to puzzle over, Jesus gives his disciples the new commandment to love: the love which Jesus has in turn received from the Father thus becomes the heritage of redeemed Christians who bring about liberation. From this love Christians are to recognize that they are happy and saved. In terms which are mysterious to us, taken from the surrounding culture, this Gospel of John does not say anything different from what the first Gospels soberly say in the supplications of the Lord's Prayer: 'Hallowed be your name, your kingdom come' among us! Justice and love among human beings constitute the honour and glory of God. The changeable love of human beings for one another is the visible manifestation, by means of the earthly signs of a loving solidarity and tenderness, of the saving event, so that in the man Jesus Christ at the same time God is recognized and human beings are sanctified. God and Jesus and human beings are all honoured! 'And the three are one.'

So this is the prophetic vision of the 'new world' of which the first reading in this liturgy speaks. It is no longer a time separate from the world in which we live: 'Behold, the dwelling of God is with men. He will dwell with them, and they shall be his people, and God himself will be with them' (Rev.21.3). Here we see the city of love, the transparent city with the gates open to the four points of the compass. There are no longer strangers or humiliated immigrants in it. All are brothers and sisters, in one love and solidarity. This is the most human final vision of that experience of faith which is historicized and has two faces in John. But the part of his provocative and stimulating message which remains alive and topical for us today is the fully Christian profession of faith according to which the majesty of God becomes visible as human salvation in the radical love of Jesus towards humanity and as a result develops from day to day, year to year around us, always. That divine majesty and that human salvation remain visible, now palpable in our midst, so that we (the ever-new generation of Christians) live on the same wavelength of love of Jesus Christ. The living human being, loving and open to others who suffer, is the honour and glory of God; all hallow his name.

The question which today's Gospel raises powerfully here and now is this: is it true that we, this year, in the midst of what is happening in our world, often far away and yet near to us, or perhaps in our neighbourhood, in our own family or community, or in our personal life, are recognizable as liberated human beings who therefore bring freedom, as those who are saved and thus bring salvation, as those who are reconciled and thus bring reconciliation?

That is the provocative message of today's Gospel.

Abba, Father, all things are possible for you (Mark 14.36)

Seventeenth Sunday in the Year (year C)
Readings: Gen.18.20-32; Luke 11.1-13
Albertinum, 26 July 1992
President of the Assembly:
Edward Schillebeeckx

Only in the two versions of the Our Father, which came into use in the early church and derives from an earlier source common to both Matthew and Luke, has the first community impressed on the memory in such a precise way the recollection of the words of Jesus about God and addressed to God. There is a third version, going back to the same period, in the non-canonical Didache, that contains the well-known liturgical addition 'For yours is the kingdom, the power and the glory...' In this prayer, like the reflection from a prism in the prayer life of his disciples, we see what moved Jesus most profoundly. Moreover this is the key to the whole of the New Testament. Here the content and the meaning of the example of Jesus (which are not directly accessible to us) are reflected and therefore become comprehensible to us too, just as the disciples followed Jesus. That is why we should note that, contrary to Matthew, Luke's account of the teaching of the Our Father by Jesus is put in a context of prayer: 'Jesus was praying in a certain place.' In this account, regardless of some possible references to a tension between the movement of John the Baptist, who taught his disciples to pray, and the first Christian movement around Jesus, it seems that Luke wants above all to say that Jesus' disciples wanted to pray as Jesus himself prayed. Hence their request to him: 'Teach us to pray.'

What we have just listened to is Luke's version of what we now call the 'Our Father', a shorter version than Matthew's which we use in our liturgy. In its effective conciseness, Luke's formula of prayer, despite its less marked Hebrew character, is perhaps closer to the words actually pronounced by Jesus, now unknown to us, which he taught above all as how we should pray.

Luke's version is above all an extremely concentrated prayer, reduced to the essentials. Knowing the Jewish tradition of prayer, we would expect the prayer to begin with solemn praise, with homage to God and exaltation of God, a doxology (as the liturgists call it), a song of praise in which the greatness of God is celebrated with a wealth of words. That is fine, but from the human point of view the persons gathered in prayer are often gratifyingly aware of being the privileged sons of this God who is praised so highly. There is nothing more subtly dangerous! Jesus looks with suspicion on an excess of self-glorification on the part of those who know that they are lovingly cared for by God. This becomes the source of many mystifications (as is suggested by the context in which Matthew puts the 'Our Father': Matt.6.5-13; cf. Luke 18.11).

Let's forget them for a moment, and let the women present here also forget the legitimate feminist question about the patriarchal character of the opening, 'Father', which is conditioned by the culture of the time. Why not equally 'Mother'? But let's forget this for the moment. The problem can be resolved only from the text itself, but this certainly doesn't justify the historical religious abuse of the term 'father'.

The Aramaic word 'Abba' can be translated most precisely as 'Dear father'. However, it is a misunderstanding to think that the term 'father' which occurs here denotes the proper name of God, as if it were the word 'father' which had to be hallowed. 'Hallowed be the name of God' is a common expression. The 'name' or the 'holiness' of God is as it were the external aspect of God who reveals himself, which faithfully respects what takes place in the unfathomable depths of the 'interiority' of God. In this sense the 'name' is the term which denotes God himself in his inscrutable mysterious existence in which, through his splendour, he fills the earth, history and humankind, and must be recognized by us precisely there. This is often very difficult in our concrete historical situation, charged with so much injustice, and which, precisely because of this, proves contrary to the splendour of the name of God. To recognize the name of God 'in our time' is no small enterprise: at a time in which incomprehensible events are taking place in former Yugoslavia and elsewhere, and also in this hard winter of the church.

The name of God is the very essence of God: his being God, whose very name must be hallowed (Ezek. 26.22-28; cf. II Sam.6.2; Jer.7.11; Amos 9.12). To 'hallow the name' has the same meaning as to 'exalt the name' (cf. Isa.59.18; Zech.14.9) or to make it 'public'. It is all about taking the holy or incomparable God seriously. The request 'to hallow the name of God' is a request addressed to our deepest faithfulness. In other words, whom do we choose in the end?

On the other hand, the term 'father' (and to be precise, let us say in the social and cultural context of the time of Jesus) only says something about the reciprocal and changing relationship of Jesus and his disciples towards God. For all his majesty, God is a mystery to whom one can turn, a very personal 'You'. Although he is above human beings, it is nevertheless possible to identify him with what we can best experience in a parent, i.e. paternal or maternal love. The Jewish kinship relationships, where they were successful and happy (think of the Jewish commandment 'Honour your father and mother') are presented here as a model of the relationship between the disciples of Jesus and God. So, says Jesus, the best thing is to turn to God as 'dear father', even if every Jewish believer knows that the father's will is law. That is why the prayer in Luke does not contain the supplication that we find in Matthew, 'Your will be done on earth as it is in heaven'. The formula 'father' already contains this thought; it is not necessary to express it further.

What is characteristic of the particular Christianity of the whole of the Our Father is that is is framed in supplications, petitions; it is not mystical contemplation. Luke emphasizes this again: 'Ask and it will be given to you; seek and you will find; knock and it will be opened to you.' With two exceptions (Matt.11.25 and John 11.41), all Jesus' prayers in the New Testament are petitions: there is no mysticism, no doxology. Jesus turns to God in supplication. For him it is not in fact humiliating to have to ask

God for something, like, 'Father, remove this cup from me', just as we often have to pray 'O God, not this!' Therefore long complicated words are no use in addressing God. Rather, it is better to do what children do, to ask and ask again, to go on until you get something. We heard the same sort of thing in the first reading, when Abraham openly supplicates God by bartering and negotiating with him: 'Will you pardon the sinful city if there are fifty righteous people in it? Even if there are only forty?' And finally he asks insistently, almost impertinently '...and if there are only ten?' and God replies, 'Yes!'

But in all these supplications there is the one universal, radical demand, which has two faces: 'Hallowed by your name' and 'Your kingdom come'. Exegetes learnedly call the construction of such a phrase the 'theological passive', that is, a construction in the passive form in which there is no mention of the name of God, though God himself is nevertheless the subject of the phrase. It is as if to say that only God can hallow his own name, act as God ('I will sanctify my great name', as we read in Ezekiel 36.23). Furthermore only God can bring in his kingdom; in the best of cases we are only useless servants. Let God be God: the one who asserts his own majesty and also the one who by reinforcing his own action and his own kingdom among human beings leads men and women themselves to fulfilment. In short, it is a matter of the honour of God and human happiness. God stakes his honour on the happiness and holiness of human beings: this is the scope of the whole of the Our Father as a petition or prayer of supplication. We supplicate God to turn towards human beings. We supplicate God that we may be capable of desiring him in all things. Obviously we cannot do this by ourselves. Perhaps in practice we do not even want to. We do not in fact ask to desire only God; there are also many good, true and dear things outside God, all external and limited aspects of the universal goodness, truth and love of God. In the Our Father we ask God to realize for us his kingdom and his being as God. That is what happens. Do we really succeed in praying in this way? This is precisely what Jesus is asking. Despite, or better thanks to the true formulation of this prayer as a supplication or 'demand' (this way of praying is the oldest Christian mysticism, which Eckhard also called 'abandonment'), we ask to be capable of leaving space for God as God. Mysticism and human salvation are the fruits of a prayer of supplication to God and not so much the result of a liberation of self, or an ascesis or a spiritual exercise. This is the way in which Jesus teaches Christians to pray.

So in the Our Father two interests are in play, that of God and that of human beings. We find two prayers related to the first aspect. With the words 'Hallowed be your name' and 'Your kingdom come', Christians who pray express as a profound essence of their preoccupation and vital interest something that is closest to the heart of God himself, specifically that God should be God and should realize himself in his intangible holiness, in human beings, in nature, in history, throughout creation. And at the same time we ask that this inviolable and majestic God shall be a God of human beings and strengthen his reign of freedom, of justice, of love and mercy among human beings. This is a divine and royal government above all human relationships, a policy and an action in which both God and human beings can realize themselves and finally achieve happiness – each confirming the other so that both are happy. It seems to me a peculiarity of Christianity that both God and human beings are happy together.

We find a triple prayer in connection with the second aspect. With the words 'Give us today our daily bread – forgive us our debts – do not lead us into temptation', Christians who pray present God with a deeply human supplication. Thus, just as we first asked that what is closest to God's heart should also become our most initimate desire, in the second part of the Our Father we ask God in his turn to take to heart what we, above all the poorest among us, regard as of vital importance: to have what we need to live, day after day (at that time in Palestine daily needs were three slim loaves of bread) and to be freed from the weight of sin which disturbs our daily existence, a debt from which God frees us if we pardon the debts of others (asking God's forgiveness cannot be separated from a human readiness to forgive). Finally, there is a prayer of supplication against the possible threat of despair: we ask to be able to continue to believe in life to the foundations, despite everything. In fact we ask not to find ourselves in the dangerous situation of losing a basic trust in life; ours may be a weak human trust, but it ultimately finds a secure base in faith in Jesus Christ, the Lord and 'author of life' (Acts 3.15). So we ask not to betray the Christian faith, in times which are hostile to the church and the world, 'times of messianic pangs' as Holy Scripture puts it (Luke says *peirasmos*).

In the relationship of covenant and love between God and human beings, what counts with God is for him to be recognized in the holiness of his name until the coming of his kingdom among human beings; for Christians, it is also a question which relates to their fellow men and women, since their interests also concern God and are connected with God's will to salvation. In this way we human beings can experience authentic love, which is shared responsibility for the good and the salvation of the other, a participation in the demands of others, which are always so varied. It could not be otherwise, and our relationship with God can only be this. For Luke that means praying in this way. Regardless of what God is asked, he will give his Holy Spirit and thus will hear every prayer. That is the meaning of the 'Our Father', which Jesus himself taught us.